Sub-Saharan Africa's Development Challenges

Sub-Saharan Africa's Development Challenges

A Case Study of Rwanda's Post-Genocide Experience

Oscar Kimanuka

palgrave
macmillan

First published in 2009 by PALGRAVE MACMILLAN® in the United States—a division of St. Martin's Press LLC, 175 Fifth Avenue, New York, NY 10010.

Where this book is distributed in the UK, Europe and the rest of the world, this is by Palgrave Macmillan, a division of Macmillan Publishers Limited, registered in England, company number 785998, of Houndmills, Basingstoke, Hampshire RG21 6XS.

Palgrave Macmillan is the global academic imprint of the above companies and has companies and representatives throughout the world.

Palgrave® and Macmillan® are registered trademarks in the United States, the United Kingdom, Europe and other countries.

ISBN-13: 978-0-230-60656-2
ISBN-10: 0-230-60656-3

Library of Congress Cataloging-in-Publication Data

Kimanuka, Oscar.
Sub-Saharan Africa's development challenges : a case study of Rwanda's post-genocide experience/ by Oscar Kimanuka.
p. cm.
Includes bibliographical references and index.
ISBN 0-230-60656-3
1. Economic development—Political aspects—Africa, Sub-Saharan—Case studies. 2. Institution building—Africa, Sub-Saharan—Case studies. 3. Africa, Sub-Saharan—Politics and government—1960—Case studies. 4. Economic development—Political aspects—Rwanda. 5. Institution building—Rwanda. 6. Administrative agencies—Rwanda—Management. 7. Civil service reform—Rwanda. 8. Rwanda—Economic policy. 9. Rwanda—Politics and government—1994– I. Title.

HC800.K563 2008
338.967571—dc22 2008027045

A catalogue record of the book is available from the British Library.

Design by Scribe Inc.

First edition: January 2009

10 9 8 7 6 5 4 3 2 1

Printed in the United States of America.

All photos courtesy of the Rwanda Investment and Export Promotion Agency.

In memory of all those who sacrificed their lives for the liberation of our motherland for the sake of posterity.

Contents

Acknowledgments

Writing this book arose from a deep conviction to share a perspective on Africa's development challenges in general and Rwanda's unique post-genocide experience in particular. By coming to terms with the unspeakable crime of genocide, the people of Rwanda have demonstrated that humanity has the courage and imagination to triumph and live beyond the unimaginable. In doing research on which this work draws, I enjoyed support from a number of friends and colleagues. I am particularly grateful to Professors Rocha Chimera and Francis Imbuga for their unwavering support, Dr. Adams Oloo for his help in discussing the contents of this book, Stephen Buckingham for his knack for details and proofreading skills, Muramira Gashegu for his research contribution on Rwanda's justice system, the Gacaca courts and Rwanda's investment opportunities, and to Palgrave for making my dream of publishing come true. I thank Jim Wallace for checking the final draft of the book before submission to my publisher and Collison Lore for his invaluable assistance with his IT skills. My contact with Palgrave started with their sister publisher, Macmillan, in Kigali. I thank Arthur Barigye, their Rwandan manager, for introducing me to them and to the world of publishing. I am indebted to Oscar Breckmans Bahizi, alumnus of Manchester University, where I cut my teeth in the world of development in the late 1990s. I am grateful to Buyela Wephukhulu, a senior consultant and researcher in development, with versatile experience in East and Central Africa's educational and human resource needs. His advice on Rwanda's challenges in education and human resources was invaluable. I am indebted to Innocent Nkurunziza, the Rwanda Bureau of Information Head of Technical Services for the help provided in IT and the patience demonstrated in the course of finalizing the book.

Finally, I am indebted to my wife, Elizabeth Kimanuka, and our children Felista Mubyeyi Kimanuka, Vincent Nyarwaya Kimanuka, Derrick Kimanuka, and Raymond Kimanuka, for their understanding, moral support, and love shown in the course of writing this book.

Abbreviations and Acronyms

APRM	African Peer Review Mechanism
CAPMER	Center for the Support of Small and Medium-sized Enterprises
CDF	Common Development Fund
CHOGM	Commonwealth Heads of Government Meeting
CSR	Civil Service Reform
DMU	Decentralization Management Unit
DFID	Department for International Development
EAC	East African Community
EDPRS	Economic Development for Poverty Reduction Strategy
FRW	Rwandan Francs
GDP	Gross Domestic Product
GOR	Government of Rwanda
HDA	Human Development Agency
HDI	Human Development Index
IC	Industrial Class
ICT	Information and Communication Technology
ILO	International Labor Organization
IMF	International Monetary Fund
JETRO	Japan External Trade Organization
LG	Local Government
MDG	Millennium Development Goal
METI	Ministry of Economy Trade and Industry (Japan)
MIFOTRA	Ministry of Public Service and Labor
MINALOC	Ministry of Local Government, Community Development, and Social Affairs
MINECOFIN	Ministry of Finance and Economic Planning
MINIJUST	Ministry of Justice
MINEDUC	Ministry of Education
MINISANTE	Ministry of Health
MININTER	Ministry of Internal Security
MOU	Memorandum of Understanding
MTEF	Medium-Term Expenditure Framework

NEPAD	New Partnership for Africa's Development
NGO	Nongovernmental Organization
NICI	National Information and Communications Infrastructure
NIRP	National Institutional Renewal Program
NPM	New Public Management
NRM	National Resistance Movement
OECD	Organization of European Economic Development
OPEC	Organization of the Petroleum Exporting Countries
PFP	Policy Framework Paper
PRGF	Poverty Reduction and Growth Facility
PRSP	Poverty Reduction Strategy Program/Paper
PSO	Public Sector Organization
PSR	Public Sector Reform
PWC	Post-Washington Consensus
RALGA	Rwanda Association of Local Government Authority
RIEPA	Rwanda Investment, Export, and Promotion Agency
RNE	Royal Netherlands Embassy
RRA	Rwanda Revenue Authority
SAP	Structural Adjustment Program
SC	Subordinate Class
SIDA	Swedish International Development Agency
SSA	Sub-Saharan Africa
SOE	State-Owned Enterprise
TICAD (IV)	Tokyo International Conference on African Development
UNDP	United Nations Development Program
UNRISD	United Nations Research Institute for Social Development
USAID	United States Agency for International Development
VERS	Voluntary Early Retirement Scheme
WAEMA	West African Economic and Monetary Union
WB	World Bank

Preface

This book aims to examine various aspects of development challenges facing sub-Saharan Africa today and attempts to provide an insight into Rwanda's postgenocide experience, taking public sector reforms as an aspect. Sub-Saharan Africa, comprising some of the poorest countries in the world, has encountered a series of development challenges arising from poor management of their economies and a deficit in governance and externally related forces, notably globalization. These countries have initiated reforms aimed at improving delivery of services critically vital to their socioeconomic development. The reforms have largely been externally driven with assistance from mainly international financial institutions and donor countries, now fashionably referred to as development partners.

Many a time, the recipient countries have not had much say in the decisions affecting disbursement of aid from the donor nations including the multilateral institutions. But now multilateral and other agencies are increasingly aware that replacing "'structural adjustment 'lending" by "'development policy 'lending" on the part of the World Bank in 2004 constituted a turning point.[1] This is opposed to the "'giver knows 'all" paradigm. This book examines the emerging nature of the of the public sector in the twenty-first century that has witnessed the disappearance of boundaries between the unfreezing of the public and private sector, resulting in what is now referred to as the Public-Private Partnership. In this environment, the traditional view of public sector administration is increasingly being challenged. It is not uncommon, even in Africa today, to find non-government and private sector agencies competing for the right to deliver services to the public sector.

Despite the reform initiatives, however, there is still inefficiency in the delivery of public services in many sub-Saharan African countries. Some of the measures pursued to improve service delivery have ranged from decentralization, privatization, performance-based contracts, Rapid Results Initiatives, and others. Some of the most serious challenges facing sub-Saharan Africa today include corruption, inadequate resources for financing government development programs, and institutional incapacity, just to mention but a few. There is need for a fundamental turnaround in attitude and behavior in decision making, or systems of delegation, without merely changing organograms and procedures that may have little or no impact on the performance of public servants.

As a way of charting her development agenda, Rwanda's reform program is premised on Vision 2020, the country's blueprint for development. In this vision, Rwanda seeks to become a medium-income country operating in a knowledge-based economy, using Information and Communication Technology (ICT) to achieve this ambition. Rwanda's development is dependent on the capacity and skills of her human resource base coupled with an efficient public sector working closely with a private sector, the future engine of the country's development. The discussion of the reforms in this study takes cognisance of the period prior to 1994 that traces the genesis of the reform program. The study further examines the period between 1995 and part of 2007, during which time the country's reconstruction and development programs were carried out.

In examining Rwanda's case, this study relies on current policy documents from the Government of Rwanda (GOR), especially the Ministries of Public Service and Labor (MIFOTRA), Ministry of Finance and Economic Planning (MINECOFIN), Civil Service Reform (CSR) reports, various government institutions and departments, newspaper articles, interviews with senior government officials, and others in the private and civil society sectors as well as a number of publications relevant to the study.

The role of the state is critically examined, and the public sector is viewed as being continuously under pressure to adopt a private sector style of management with the task of delivering better services to the citizens of Rwanda. This study critically examines whether or not the changes introduced have produced results in solving the country's socioeconomic challenges facing sub-Saharan Africa in general and Rwanda in particular and also examines the role of education and training as well as ICT in the country's socioeconomic transformation. This study observes that while Rwanda has made impressive strides in her socioeconomic recovery, a number of hurdles remain for her to achieve her goal of becoming a medium income economy operating on a knowledge-based economy. Rwanda's inspiration is drawn from small countries like Singapore and Mauritius that have no known natural resources but have used their human resource base to turn around the fortunes of their economies. In the case of Rwanda, just like these countries, it is leadership that has been a source of inspiration and guidance.

The targeted audience for this study includes the civil society, academia, development partners, schools and other institutions of higher learning, and a host of others interested in postconflict recovery and development. Despite a harrowing story, Rwanda seems to be providing a guide to a number of countries emerging from conflict, including Southern Sudan, Liberia, Sierra Leone, and others, as demonstrated by high-level visits from these 'countries' policy makers and political leaders.

1

Introduction

> Today's development economics is like eighteenth century medicine . . . when impoverished countries have pledged [for help, the main] prescription has been budgetary tightening for patients much too poor to own our belts.
>
> —*Jeffrey Sachs, 2005*

Background to the Sub-Saharan Development Challenges

This book attempts to analyze sub-Saharan African development challenges with an insight into Rwanda's post genocide experience from 1994 to 2007. The challenges include the introduction of Public Sector

Figure 1.1 Banks located in the Kigali business center.

Reform (PSR) programs that were initiated more than a decade ago, and this book gives a specific case study of Rwanda's own experience that could be shared by other countries emerging from conflict to development. The book takes into account various externally driven forces, including globalization, which has forced a reinvention of the relationship between the public and private sectors (Grundberg 1998, 591–605).

Globalization has contributed, considerably in many sub-Saharan African countries, including Rwanda, to a fiscal squeeze that has increased difficulties in the raising of revenue and has enhanced the demands for public expenditure (Grundberg 1998, 591–605). The enormity of the challenges that faced Rwanda following the events of 1994 and the attempts to rebuild an infrastructure and public sector that were destroyed are discussed. It is hoped that this book will make a modest but significant contribution to lessons in post conflict reconstruction in developing countries, particularly Africa.

Numerous studies have been conducted on the development challenges facing sub-Saharan Africa today, but they have mainly dealt with the effects of structural adjustment programs "but almost without exception, concentrated on macroeconomics: effects on government revenues and expenditures, imports, exports and the balance of payments, output, income and growth" (Enos 1995, xiv). As shown in this book, the future of sub-Saharan Africa will be greatly influenced by technical progress that they achieve, which, in turn, will depend on their relative success in advancing their science and technology (Enos 1995, xiv). While disease, civil war, and government failure define Africa's present, Information and Communication Technology (ICT)—applied intelligently and fairly—could bolster our region's future to an unprecedented degree.[1]

It is hoped that policy makers will find this book beneficial to them, especially in countries that have faced similar challenges of development, and it is hoped that this book shall inform their efforts at reversing past setbacks and securing renewed development in the coming decades (Belshaw and Livingstone 2002).

The 1980s and part of the 1990s were periods of deepening economic crisis for sub-Saharan Africa. In fact, some observers have referred to this period as "a lost decade" The international economic environment became increasingly hostile, particularly with declining terms of trade leading to heavy servicing of debts (Kirkpatrick 1995, 285–98). In view of the economic crisis, it was acknowledged that Africa's structure of production and export trade had to respond to the prevailing patterns of global trade and production that took place during the said period. As a result of these and other concerns, sub-Saharan African countries undertook economic policy reform and trade liberalization programs that aimed at introducing structural changes in domestic production and external trade (Kirkpatrick

1995, 285–98). The idea behind these changes was to stimulate growth and improve conditions for long-term social and economic development. The world recession of the 1970s and 1980s, arising from the escalation of oil prices by the Organization of the Petroleum Exporting Countries (OPEC), was a major factor that contributed to the poor performance of Africa's economies. The structural adjustment programs introduced, as a remedy by the World Bank (WB) and the International Monetary Fund (IMF), for the African countries included the following:

- Drastic reduction of trade barriers protecting the local economy from foreign competition
- Deep reduction or elimination of subsidies and price controls, which "distorted" internal prices for a number of goods and services
- Restructuring of the financial system and weakening or removal of controls on the movement of capital
- Privatization of state-controlled firms
- Elimination of control on private foreign investment
- Reduction of the role of the state, not only in the economy, but also in the provision of social services

Among development analysts and policy makers in both the developed and developing countries, there had also been a major review of what constituted development and policies for meeting these challenges to development. It was widely agreed that rapid economic growth in sub-Saharan Africa left far too many people still trapped in "absolute poverty."[2]

The book also delves into the period prior to the 1994 events in Rwanda. This is an attempt to provide a background to the reform program against a backdrop of harrowing challenges that beset policy makers prior to and after the 1994 genocide. The calamity of the genocide threw the entire socioeconomic and political institutions into limbo.

This book highlights the various policy instruments with the intent of bringing Rwanda's socioeconomic development priorities in line with the country's Vision 2020. The realization of that vision is premised on the availability of a well-trained and motivated public sector workforce that is dedicated to delivering quality and results-oriented service alongside a private sector that is seen as the future engine of the country's development. Rwanda's public sector program is rooted in the structural adjustment program of the Bretton Woods Institutions of the WB and the IMF that characterized many of sub-Saharan PSR programs during the 1980s and the 1990s and, to some extent, the 2000s.

According to the Rwanda Ministry of Public Service and Labor (MIFOTRA) policy framework for Rwanda's CSR program (2002, 2), this PSR program is in line with the concern for good governance and is a continuous management process designed to bring about efficiency in public institutions and specialized bodies.

The reform should also help the government to build a civil service that can satisfy the basic needs of the people of Rwanda and contribute to their well-being. It is recognized, in the said policy document that the civil service is the driving force behind the socioeconomic development of the country, especially as it plays a unique role in the following ways:

- Ensuring compliance with laws and regulations while looking after the smooth running of the government machinery within the civil service ambit
- Initiating management policies for the different government departments
- Working out management norms and procedures to be followed in the various areas of civil service
- Carrying out supervision and control of government human resource management, including control of the quality of services offered to the public
- Carrying out training, education, and information for the benefit of the population in its development activities
- Setting up policies and programs relating to the various sectors of development

The Rwanda government's current reform program phase is referred to as "Rwanda Public Sector Transformation and Reconfiguration." This program falls under the country's ongoing socioeconomic and political administrative reforms on one hand and the dynamics of good governance on the other, in the context of the Millennium Development Goals, whose aim is sustainable economic growth for the country. The reforms come at an opportune time to reinforce the measures taken by the government with the aim of boosting the country's economic development in the context of Vision 2020.

The reforms also arise from the conviction by the government of Rwanda (GOR) that in the absence of an effective public sector, it would be difficult, if not impossible, to effectively deliver public services to the people. Related to the PSR is the attempt to create an enabling environment for the growth and sustainability of the private sector, civil society, and increased domestic and foreign investment.

Challenges of the Reform Program

Public sector reform program, sometimes referred to as Civil Service Reforms (CSR), introduced in sub-Saharan Africa in the 1980s "remained hindered by a myriad of factors including lack of efficiency, lack of accountability, ineffective management practices, and corruption."[3] In the 1990s, the reforms were made broader by focusing closely on the role of the state, an assessment of government functions beyond the policy and reverse centralization, a feature of postcolonial administrative setup.

Neoliberal economic policies of the WB, IMF, and donor countries were introduced as part of the package of the reform program in sub-Saharan African countries. While developing countries have taken up reforms at various stages, there has not been considerable progress with regard to efficient delivery of public services. The few that have had some level of success have been due to a favorable political environment that provides the power base, incentives, and commitment to implement often difficult and challenging reforms.

This modest scale of implementation of New Public Management (NPM; McCourt 2002) has posed challenges to the realization of socio-economic development in a number of developing countries, including sub-Saharan Africa. This study highlights the difficulties of introducing reforms and how countries adopting those reforms are coping to meet the needs of governments and their political contexts. The introduction of the

Figure 1.2 Kigali City's main roundabout.

reforms in Rwanda has been more daunting, in view of a challenging history, particularly the consequences of the 1994 genocide.

The WB and other donors have focused their attention on "finding alternative ways of organizing and managing the public services and redefining the role of the state to give more prominence to markets and competition, and to the private and voluntary sectors." It should be pointed out that the public service "has always been the tool available to African governments for the implementation of development goals and objectives. It is seen as a pivot for growth of the African economies" (McCourt 2002).

However, the central governments in sub-Saharan Africa are already overextended to the extent that there has been urgent need to reengineer their roles and functions. There is need for creating an enabling environment that includes, among other things, incentives for performance for the improvement of macroeconomic stability and efficiency. The NPM style of reforms is based on performance incentives "and the disciplines that exist in a market environment" (McCourt 2002). However, for a country that has had a post genocide challenge of rebuilding from scratch a civil service that collapsed in 1994, this constitutes a monumental challenge.

It is against this background that, it is hoped, the experiences of developing countries, especially Rwanda, will provide some useful lessons in the effective delivery of public services in Africa. The development of a strong civil service in Rwanda is seen as "a matter of primordial importance to achieve the economic recovery of those priority areas marked out for poverty alleviation" (MIFOTRA 2002, 3). It is important to recognize that the vulnerability of Rwanda's economy following the severe socioeconomic consequences of the 1994 genocide and the introduction of Neoliberal reforms created far reaching consequences to the public sector, especially the civil service. Many retrenched civil servants have not had sufficient packages to take care of their families. Some of them have gone back to school, and others have been retrained in tertiary institutions. Fewer of the retrenched civil servants have been absorbed in self-employment and the private sector. Rwanda's private sector is still small in comparison with those in the East African region.

This study, therefore, aims at explaining, among other things, the challenges encountered by sub-Saharan African countries in general in their PSR programs, and in particular, Rwanda's own experience in view of her unique recent history. A key recommendation will be what Rwanda's experience has to offer to developing countries, particularly in Africa, where many people are still grappling with socioeconomic problems.

Objectives of the Study

This study seeks to explore the challenges encountered by Rwanda with a view to assessing the effectiveness of the PSRs. The study specifically seeks to accomplish the following:

- Assess the PSR measures introduced in Rwanda from 1995 to 2005
- Evaluate the effectiveness of the reform program and what lessons can be learned from Rwanda's own experience

Why Public Sector Reforms?

The subject of PSRs in sub-Saharan Africa has elicited considerable debate in the last twenty years. "However, most of the recent reforms, under the influence of the New Public Management (NPM), have been driven by a combination of economic, social, political and technological factors, which have triggered the quest for efficiency and for ways to cut the cost of delivering public services."[4]

Rwanda's recent experience at reforms in the public sector continues to generate interest in academic and donor circles, particularly in view of bold measures taken at policy level. The GOR's reform program "is in line with the concern for good governance, as it is a continuous management process, designed to bring about public service efficiency in ministries, public institutions and specialised bodies" (MIFOTRA 2002, 2).

Through this study, it is hoped that considerable information will be provided on the ongoing PSRs in Rwanda, whose reform program appears to be ambitious and is in line with the country's development goals and Vision 2020. Further, this book will provide a useful guide to policy makers in post conflict situations that require bold initiatives, supported by a favorable political environment. It is hoped that the study will further contribute to the existing body of literature on the challenges encountered by policy makers in the PSR programs in Africa.

This book offers lessons in post conflict management of national affairs, and will hopefully be a useful guide to policy makers and all those involved in public policy formulation particularly with regard to CSR programs. Conducting a study on public sector reform programs on a country like Rwanda, which emerged from the horrors of genocide barely thirteen years ago, is fraught with challenges and difficulties, particularly with respect to getting readily available data and information for use. Nevertheless, the importance of such a study cannot be gainsaid.

For the last thirteen years, the country has steadily come to the limelight as one that has made significant strides in nation building, particularly with respect to building institutions and mechanisms that have contributed to steady macroeconomic stability in a post conflict context.

Literature Review

There is a considerable body of literature on PSR program in developing countries, particularly sub-Saharan Africa. In the case of this book, the literature to be reviewed focuses mainly on secondary sources—published material from the public sector management, organizational development policy statements, and newspaper articles. The idea is to analyze the gradual shift from the government's bureaucratic style of management to the NPM style and to private sector management style.

Hood (1991), in Public Sector Management Reforms in Africa, a study commissioned by the Economic Commission for Africa,[5] indicates that the major NPM doctrine encompasses the following:

- Direct public sector costs cut and labor discipline raised so as to improve resource use
- Private-sector-style management practices applied to increase flexibility in decision making
- Competition in the public sector (through term contracts and tendering) increased, as rivalry is the key to lower costs and better standards
- The public sector disaggregated and decentralized to make units more manageable and to increase competition among them
- Controls shifted from inputs to outputs, to stress results rather than procedure
- Explicit standards and performance measures established, because accountability requires clearly stated aims whereas efficiency requires attention to goals
- Managers given powers to conduct hands-on professional management, because accountability requires clear assignment of responsibility, not diffusion of power

The challenge facing sub-Saharan Africa has been linked to a socioeconomic situation that has been degenerating while, at the same time, the external environment has not been conducive enough. The environment has not been facilitative, and at the same time, bureaucracy has tended to further exacerbate the crisis. This has compromised the capacity of the state to deliver services to the people (Grindle and Thomas 1991). As can be deduced from the preceding, the main purpose of the PSR is the improvement of the performance of the civil service. The aim of this is to raise the quality of public services for the purpose of enhancing the capacity to perform government core functions in the interest of uplifting the socioeconomic welfare of the people of sub-Saharan Africa, in general, and Rwanda in particular.

Sub-Saharan Africa is approximately 2.6 times the size of the United States, and it is a common error to lump all of these countries together into one basket (Awed 1998, 1). The fifty-two countries differ in many aspects, ranging from territorial size, climate, natural resources, populations, and socioeconomic conditions.

Despite the foregoing, there are a number of similarities among countries constituting sub-Saharan Africa. For instance, the region has registered high population growth rates. According to the WB, fertility rates in sub-Saharan Africa are higher than in any developing part of the world, including those countries with comparable levels of income, education, and life expectancy (WB 1997). Furthermore, the populations of African countries, along those of South Asia, remain among the poorest in the world. For instance, on average 45 to 50 percent of Africans live below the poverty line. Economic growth and financial stability have continued to dodge most of sub-Saharan Africa over the last ten or so years. Between 1988 and 1992, Africa's gross domestic product (GDP) growth rate was increasing on modest levels, but per capita growth was neutralized by high population growth, which, for the majority of countries, resulted in negative GDP per capita growth (WB 1996).

Origins of the Economic Crisis in Sub-Saharan Africa

Some of the reasons advanced for sub-Saharan Africa's general problems of underdevelopment are linked to the legacies bequeathed by the twin evils of slave trade and colonialism. But the actual genesis of the crisis of the 1980s largely stems from the events of the 1970s when the oil-importing countries were faced with a large balance of trade deficits arising from the high oil prices of 1973 to 1974 (Awed 1998).

What came to be known as "the oil shock" of 1973 to 1974 led to the sudden rise in the price of crude petroleum by OPEC that caused a severe economic recession in the so-called developing countries, more especially in sub-Saharan Africa, with far-reaching consequences. Some of these consequences included high interest rates, falling investment rates, rising inflation, general economic stagnation, and widespread unemployment. "The economic prospects of heavily indebted countries no longer appeared viable to the commercial banks, and they ceased virtually all voluntary lending to developing countries by mid-1980s" (Awed 1998).

The Berg Report, according to Peter Lawrence (2002, 51), set out what became the orthodox explanation of the causes of sub-Saharan African economic stagnation during the 1970s. By the end of the 1970s, it was clear that much of the continent was suffering from increasing balance of payments and domestic budget deficits as well as falling or stagnating growth rates of agricultural and industrial production, which left many countries inevitably seeking help from the Bretton Woods Institutions. It is interesting to observe that while African governments essentially saw the cause of their economic decline as related to their inequitable economic relations with the developed world, the analysis of Berg and his colleagues argued that despite these problems, the root causes could be found in domestic policies of the African countries (Lawrence 2002, 51).

The Intervention of the WB and IMF

The late Tanzanian president Mwalimu Julius Kambarage Nyerere was less charitable about the IMF's role in Africa's development efforts. This was partly due to the impatience he and other Africans had especially with regard to the austerity measures that the Fund demanded in exchange for its loans. Nyerere once called the IMF a "substitute for colonialism," charging that it and other international financial institutions, such as the WB, had become "tools of the rich nations to control the economies of the poor nations."[6] In a hard-hitting article published in a leading Ugandan newspaper, Dr. Tajudeen Abdulrahman, who works with the African Union, says that "in the case of the IMF and the WB, the convention is that the Europeans get to nominate who heads the former and their American cousins choose the latter" (2007).

As a result of deepening economic crisis in sub-Saharan Africa in the 1980s, the WB and the IMF introduced structural adjustment programs (SAPs) as "a condition for getting new loans from these two international financial institutions . . . for the implementation of SAPs" (2007). The intervention of SAPs was to stimulate economic growth through the consolidation of capitalism. SAPs promoted a whole range of reforms based on restructuring the economies of many sub-Saharan African countries. A key objective of the reform program was to ensure that the recipient country's economies became market-oriented through the encouragement of export-based growth. This neoliberal economic philosophy was behind the SAPs. This philosophy ensured that the recipient economy would be efficient, healthy, and productive in the long run if market forces were allowed to operate with minimum government intervention.

Consequently, "the role and institutional character of the state has been questioned, and the public sector has been under pressure to adopt private sector orientation."[7]

The Introduction of the Public Sector Reforms

The WB and other donor agencies have from the 1980s, and more recently, been "concerned with finding alternative ways of organizing and managing the public services and redefining the role of the state to give more prominence to markets and competition and to the private and voluntary sector" (2007). The first set of reforms introduced in the 1980s mainly focused on "cutting down to size," following the structural adjustment programs supported by the WB and the IMF. The emphasis in these reforms was on controlling salary costs primarily through job reduction. This led to the retrenchment of civil servants. The second stage of the reforms began in the 1990s and presented a broad range of reforms that aimed at "performance assessment, monitoring, transparency, benchmarking, decentralization, regulation, and sound financial management.

The second form of reforms, the NPM, has its roots in Western developed countries, mainly the United Kingdom and the United States. The development of a new approach to public sector management arose from the need to reinvent government by adopting "private sector concepts and styles, the adoption of quasi-markets and contracting processes and application of explicit standards and measures of performance" (McHugh 1997, 433). Reinvention of government meant a "fundamental transformation of public systems and organizations to unprecedented increases in their efficiency, effectiveness, adaptability, and capacity to innovate" (Obongo 2000). However, the new public management is not just about efficiency; it also "involves ideas of democratic participation, as well as accountability and empowerment. There is also constant tension between two main themes: making government efficient and keeping government accountable" (Minogue 1998a).

The introduction of modern, public sector reforms in sub-Saharan Africa arose from "a common response to common pressures namely public hostility to government, shrinking budgets and imperatives of globalisation" (Polidano 1999). The new PSRs emanated from external pressure, through the SAPs. The bilateral and multilateral donors "have extended economic into political conditionality, embracing both public management change and democratisation" (Minogue 1998b, 2). Part of the strategy of implementation of the reforms in the public sector was to transform the existing traditional machinery of administration through the modernization of the public service "through external inducement, transfer of technology and training by foreign experts" (Dwivedi and Neff 1982, 63). It is significant to observe though that there is no universal model of reform (McCourt 2002). What is important is the institutional and political context of the reform program.

According to Stevens and Teggemann (2006), countries like Botswana, Ghana, Tanzania, Kenya, Zambia, and Rwanda have all embarked on comparable reform paths and have showed different results. Botswana and Tanzania have proved to be the most progressive reformers and have made promising progress in introducing a comprehensive set of reforms. Part of the reasons for the success in those countries has been a result of a favorable political environment that has provided the power base, incentives, and commitment to implement reforms even during difficult circumstances (Stevens and Teggemann 2006). Furthermore, the components of the program introduced have been appropriately tailored to the countries' context and strategically sequenced. Willy McCourt (2002) poses the question as to why the scale of the implementation of the NPM in sub-Saharan Africa and in other developing countries has been rather modest.

This work highlights the importance of adopting the NPM model to meet the needs of governments and their political contexts with special reference to Rwanda's case from 1995 to 2005 and underscores the challenges encountered in their implementation.

Rwanda's Public Sector Reforms

Prior to 1994, Rwanda enjoyed "substantial flows of external aid. Official development assistance grew from US$35 million between 1971 and 1974 to US$343 million between 1990 and 1993. The approach to economic development, however, lacked a focus on people, the good early performance of the economy could not be sustained, poverty increased and violence escalated" (IDA 1996, 6). In 1994, Rwanda's GDP fell by 50 percent, and almost all economic sectors collapsed. In the aftermath of the genocide, the government managed quickly to stabilize the economy and put it on a path of rapid growth (70 percent from 1994 to 1997), which was largely driven by the postconflict resumption of economic activity and services spurred by the presence of a large number of international nongovernment organizations (NGOs) and relief agencies.

The 1994 genocide marks an important watershed in the history of a country that experienced episodes of violence and centralization in the decision-making process. The period after 1994 also constitutes a transition from war to peace and from the old order in which the style of managing public affairs changed to the extent of involving citizens in matters affecting their day-to-day lives. The Rwanda government has recognized that the development of the country in the twenty-first century requires a focus on the people (WB 1999) through empowerment, broad participation, improvements in education, health and capacity building, and the meaningful employment of the people.

In the following years, the government successfully implemented a broad range of programs of economic reforms, focusing on the exchange and trade regime, privatization of state-owned enterprises, reform of public administration, budget and financial management, and private sector development. As a result of these reforms, the last ten years have experienced growth in GDP, mainly driven by agriculture and construction that have contributed 6 percent and 9 percent respectively.

At the center of the reform program is the Poverty Reduction Strategy Program (PRSP), which was completed in June 2002. In April 2005, Rwanda reached the Highly Indebted Poor Countries completion point, the decision point reached in December 2000. According to the WB,[8] significant debt relief has consolidated room for development expenditure. Efforts by government have resulted in a sound economic governance framework, including independent regulatory agencies, stronger public expenditure, management systems, independent audit agencies, and a strong focus on anticorruption policies and measures. Despite achievements, "fiscal decentralisation to local government has been relatively disappointing, with slow progress towards meeting the target of 10% of National Domestic Revenue devoted to the Common development Fund."[9]

The private sector is expected to play a crucial role in Rwanda's socioeconomic transformation. In this regard, according to the Poverty Reduction Strategy Paper (PRSP) annual report 2003 to 2004, "the measures taken in ensuring that the private sector plays its rightful role include a 'one-stop shop' for investors, a review of the investment code, restructuring for the Center for the Support of Small and Medium-sized Enterprises (CAPMER), creation of an arbitration center dealing with commercial disputes, and the establishment of a commercial chamber. The creation of a National Accounting Commission and Regulation Agency is envisaged."[10] In 2006, the GOR launched a second PRSP, which is due to be finalized in the course of 2007. This strategy, dubbed Economic Development for Poverty Reduction Strategy (EDPRS), represents a comprehensive development agenda and the need to ensure progress across both the productive and social sectors and will cover a five-year period. The EDPRS is expected to form more of an operational tool than an "aspirational vision statement and will be supported through detailed sector plans."[11] One of the ways to curb the high levels of poverty in Rwanda is through the implementation of EDPRS, which covers different micro- and macroeconomic sectors. President Paul Kagame, in a speech to mark the official launching of the EDPRS in Kigali, observed that "Rwandans need to be liberated from poverty and I wish it could be changed to poverty liberation instead of poverty reduction" (Nzaramba and Majyambere 2006).

Rwanda's PSR has attempted to enhance effectiveness across public service agencies (Nzaramba and Majyambere). Harmonization of salary levels across government agencies, including semiautonomous and government parastatals, is said to have made monetary gains for government. An important aspect of the PSR program is the capacity building program undertaken by the Human Development Agency (HIDA), which is the coordinating capacity building initiative across the central government (Nzaramba and Majyambere). The Ministry of Local Government, in line with the reform program, has developed a capacity building initiative for "citizens as well as local government authorities." Based on an assessment, it attempts "to deliver courses and review and evaluate the functioning of organs with the view to identifying further capacity building needs."

Rwanda's challenge lies in attaining and stabilizing real growth rate between 7 percent and 8 percent per annum over the next fifteen to twenty years. According to the Ministry of Finance and Economic Planning (MINECOFIN),[12] the country's medium-term macroeconomic objectives are, first, to achieve an annual, real GDP growth rate of at least 6 percent; second, to keep annual inflation at 3 percent; and third, to maintain gross international reserve equivalent to at least six months of imports.

Rwanda's Economic Performance

Between 1995 and 2001, Rwanda's GDP grew by 70 percent. According to MINECOFIN, a significant portion of that growth was a postwar normalization that has seen a 6.7 percent growth since 2001. Inflation at 64 pecent in 1994 had been reduced to developed world levels by 1998. By 2005, inflation rate had stabilized at 11 percent.[13] By the end of 2007, inflation was estimated at 10.8 percent.[14] In a budget speech in October 2007 presented to Parliament by Rwanda's Minister of Finance, Honorable James Musoni observed that the budget of the financial year 2007 through 2008 is 15 percent greater than the 2003 budget and the said budget is 607.5 billion Rwandan Francs, an increase of about 80 billion Rwandan Francs in comparison to the previous financial year. A large proportion of the increase estimated at 73 percent was allocated to the sectors of transport

Figure 1.3 The headquarters of the newly refurbished Ministry of Finance and Economic Planning.

and communications, fuel and energy, agriculture, health, and education.[15] Part of the reason for including education and health as priority areas for government arise from Rwanda's Vision 2020, which states in part that "at the core of Rwanda's development process constitutes the country's principal asset: its people. Human resources will be improved so that Rwanda can become a knowledge-based economy."[16]

The GOR believes that a climate of vibrant economic regeneration, with private sector growth, increased rural economic activity, and the creation of employment would strengthen the process of national reconciliation (WB 1999). The background to Rwanda's foundation to her economic growth is outlined in a policy framework paper (PFP) of June 1998. In this document, the reforms outlined are aimed at, among other things, maintaining macroeconomic stability and improving public resource mobilization and management. Furthermore, it aims at developing a market-based agriculture, enhancing the role of women, establishing the institutional, legal, and infrastructure framework conducive to private sector growth and external competitiveness, strengthening public institutional and administrative capacity, and improving public service delivery (WB 1999).

The improvement of public sector service delivery will need to move beyond downsizing to generate savings. It will need adequate terms and conditions for civil servants, which remain serious impediments to quality delivery of services, not only in Rwanda but also in other sub-Saharan African countries. As pointed out by the South Africa's Minister of Public

Service and Administration, "to place the African continent on the required development trajectory, reform of the public service is crucial in ensuring implementation and in creating the conducive environment for good governance and service delivery."[17]

Conceptual and Theoretical Framework

Development strategies in Africa are the by-product of a certain historical moment with its social, economic, and political conditions as well as the dominant, or leading, development thought of that moment. While the Lagos Plan of Action in 1980 was the product of state-led and collective self reliance mode of development, the New Partnership for African Development (NEPAD), which came more than twenty years later, reflects the Post-Washington Consensus (PWC) model of development. The debate within the latter mode is no longer about whether the state should intervene in the development process. It is, rather, about the ways and mechanisms of such intervention and the relationship between state, private sector, and civil society for achieving development.[18]

Yet Africa is still in a need of a new development model that provides a partnership framework between the development actors. This work uses the PWC model whose central core is derived from writings and speeches of Joseph Stiglitz, former Chief Economist of the WB and a leading critique of the Bretton Woods Institutions as well as globalization. The PWC has been celebrated for shifting to a more realistic policy framework whereby aspects of the real world, for example, market imperfections, are central to analysis rather than deviations from an unattainable equilibrium (Bayliss 2000). When it comes to privatization, the central theme of the PWC is that competition may, in fact, be more important than ownership.

However, while the PWC has been heralded as a departure from traditional economic development orthodoxy, close scrutiny reveals that there is little to distinguish PWC when it comes to policies. The PWC is welcome in that it calls for regulation at least to accompany privatization.

2

Public Sector Reform Programs in Sub-Saharan Africa

> Elephants and public organisations have something in common. Elephants are believed to be slow and insensitive creatures, when in fact they can run very fast and are very sensitive. Similarly, public organisations are believed to be low-performing and unresponsive, when in fact many public organizations perform very well and are models of responsiveness.
>
> —*Brewer and Seldon (2000, 685)*

Background to the Reforms

Today there is widespread consensus in circles of practitioners and academics that "dysfunctional" state bureaucracies constitute the biggest impediment to development (Gerhard and Anders 2005). Excessive red tape, opaque procedures, and corrupt civil servants are perceived to delay and reroute badly needed development. The WB report (1989) blames "bad governance," a bloated bureaucracy, patrimonialism, and corruption for the elusiveness of economic growth in sub-Saharan Africa in the 1980s and 1990s. In subsequent years, however, the concept of good governance was developed as a remedy to these problems. By the end of the 1990s, the concept constituted one of the central elements of international development assistance in sub-Saharan Africa (Abrahamsen 2000). Available evidence suggests that African governments have pursued political and economic reforms since the late 1980s in a bid to promote economic growth, reduce poverty, and encourage popular participation and good governance (Kayizzi-Mugerwa 2003, 1). Although many of the sub-Saharan African countries were and are still experiencing tremendous hardships with both their political systems and their bureaucracies also not delivering, very few saw or have seen the need to internally reform their systems. This is mainly so because the prereform practices across the sectors are a product of colonial practices, post colonial nation building, and the current international conventions. As it has been noted by Anders Danielson (2001), "It is something of an irony that while bureaucratic inadequacy is usually cited as a major cause of the dismal result of Africa's economic performance, these same governments are usually entrusted with implementing profound and difficult reforms in order to improve economic performance."

Undoing these has often meant a profound challenge, not only to vested interests, but also even to the composition of the state (Batley 1999). On the other hand, in Western democracies, systems of checks and balances built into government structures have formed the core of good governance and have contributed to the empowering of citizens for more than two hundred years (Anwar 2005). This chapter examines the various public sector reforms implemented in sub-Saharan Africa, the challenges encountered, and possible lessons learned.

Reforms in many cases refer to shifts in the boundary away from the state and toward the private sector, or privatization (Minogue 1998b). The balance is moving significantly away from the state provision toward market provision of goods and services. This shift represents the relative decline of the public sector and the relative growth of the private sector (Cope, Leishman, and Starie 1997). Economic crisis has not only forced change but also created stress conditions, which make resistance to change especially strong. The losses from reform for powerful groups (politicians, public sector workers, and sometimes the professionals and administrators) are more certain than the gains to an ill-served public.

In such circumstances and conditions, "the constituency for reform, in a new manager class and beneficiaries, takes time to emerge. Support for reform and especially for the losers from reform, therefore, requires long term commitment" (Batley 1999, 762). Transferring reforms thus means breaking old structures and building new ones, and this cannot be achieved in the short term as often attempted. It is a measure that requires long-term commitment and the cooperation of a wide range of stakeholders to take root.

Financial support from bilateral and multilateral institutions has been crucial for the implementation of reforms in sub-Saharan Africa. Recent assessments indicate, however, that outcomes have been far from satisfactory. Where better results have been observed, there remain serious questions of sustainability. The poor outcomes have been blamed on the weaknesses of the public sectors in Africa (Batley 1999, 1). According to their critics, African bureaucracies play a contradictory and conflict-ridden role, being, at once, part of the problem and the cure. According to Lienert (1998), Olowu (1997), and Klitgaard (1989), weak public institutions have implied loose operational guidelines for public service work while, on the other hand, poor finances have reduced incentives and morale among employees.

For African governments to benefit from economic reforms, there is need for a new modus operandi for the public sector. Distortions in its core functions must be eradicated by altering the incentive and induction systems for public employees and by changing the operation of the civil service. Furthermore, African governments need to take their reputations and credibility seriously, not only with respect to their domestic constituencies, but also in relation to the development partners. Past experience has shown that, when governments cannot be taken at their word, their policy effectiveness in fighting poverty, for instance, becomes seriously eroded (Kayizzi-Mugerwa 2001; DFID 1997).

Furthermore, when policy makers are responsible for the formulation as well as implementation of their reforms and when, moreover, they are apt to defend them before their constituencies and donor community, they are said to "own" their reforms. While the development partners keep emphasizing the importance of ownership for reform success, few African countries have been able to establish an institutional culture that is supportive of domestic reforms. The failure of economic reforms to have any lasting impact in Africa has, thus, been blamed on the lack of ownership by governments. In return, policies continue to be imposed from "above" by donors or multilateral agencies and domestically by governments themselves, without the participation of the population. This lack of ownership, according to Kayizzi (2003), can be blamed for the crisis-ridden nature of African economies.

Sub-Saharan African Public Sector Reforms

Indeed, in many of the African countries, "fire brigade" operations, supported by donors, were necessary to prevent further decline but failed to fundamentally provide the scope for ownership by domestic leaders. Africa has also lacked structures for consensus building, with political exclusion more the norm than the exception. The political environment has not adequately supported the evolution of good governance (Aron 1997; Coolidge and Rose-Ackerman 1997). The failure of policy makers to undertake measures for better public management and accountability has negatively impacted relations with the donors. Donor bureaucracies and those of multilateral agencies have exhibited a lag in adapting to the new thinking, which emphasizes partnership (Van der Heijden 2000; Asian Development Bank 1999). The threat of aid embargo is still used by donors as a disciplining device, although experiences from Kenya, Zambia, and Malawi indicate that this tends to hit the poor and vulnerable groups harder than the more affluent ones without pushing governments toward improved accountability (Bigsten and Kayizzi-Mugerwa 2000).

In a review of the African experience, Abdalla Hamdok (2003) argues that good governance is a prerequisite for sustainable development. Growth and development demand law and order, the creation of transparent and administrative structures, the extension of social infrastructure to the rural areas (Hamdok 2003), the protection of poor and vulnerable groups and their inclusion in the decision making process, and the preservation of peace and security. Hamdok concludes, however, that it is ultimately politics that determine the nature of governance. It is, therefore, important for African countries to open up their political space and exercise more inclusive politics. The best way of nurturing good governance is to let citizens participate in decisions that affect them. This is best done through devolution of power and by strengthening domestic institutions.

Tanzania

A comparative study of Ghana and Tanzania, conducted by Yvonne M. Tsikata (Hamdok 2003, 13), "provides interesting contrasts of sub-Saharan Africa's reform experience." Though the two countries are situated in politically volatile regions of the continent, they have so far managed to steer clear of political destabilization and have largely been able to introduce and maintain political pluralism (Hamdok 2003, 13). Ghana was an early reformer, starting in the 1980s, whereas Tanzania was a much later convert to the reform process, owing to the then prevailing political ideology of Ujamaa, or African socialism, introduced by the late President Julius Kambarage Nyerere, whose relations with donor agencies, particularly the WB and the IMF, were far from friendly, as noted earlier. In the later part of the 1980s, Ghana experienced significant backsliding in its reform efforts, partly owing to the policy diversion implied by the introduction of political pluralism. While the policy of state-led development was for several years supported by a number of bilateral donors, it was ostensibly slow to reform and slower still in committing to market liberalism; it is now seen as making considerable progress, nevertheless. For instance, the most critical components of the two reform programs carried out in the 1990s and in recent years "bring together the two central themes of improving the quality of public services, and building the capacity necessary to deliver these services" (Teskey and Hooper 1999).

Ghana

Ghana, like many other African countries, experienced economic crises in the 1970s and 1980s, which led her public sector to be in complete disarray by the mid-1980s. Difficult socioeconomic conditions prevailing in the country "made it extremely difficult to recruit and to retain technical and professional staff. Gradually, the bloated public sector became increasingly incapable of performing basic tasks let alone to facilitate national development. The ineffectiveness of the public sector became a serious hindrance when the government embarked on economic reforms in 1983" (Owusu 2005). Consequently, "public sector reforms became a central component of the country's adjustment and stabilisation programmes" (Gregory 1996). In 1994, Ghana changed focus of public sector reforms with the creation of the National Institutional Renewal Program (NIRP) and the launching of the Civil Service Performance Improvement Program. Like the "qualitative" second-generation reforms of the time, these programs had broader objectives that included enhancing efficiency and facilitating the development of a proactive and motivated public sector" (Gregory 1996, 11).

In October 1997, the government implemented the Public Sector Reinvention and Modernization Strategy to help transform state institutions, their accountability and performance framework, and their relationship with the private sector and civil society (Gregory 1996, 11). Owusu (2005) is of the view that, although the NIRP's Overview Reform Committee was chaired by the then Vice President, J.E.A. Mills (NIRP 1998), overall, little progress was made due to lack of political will from the former government as far as following through with the promised reform. A recent evaluation of the reforms has concluded that " . . . on the whole, the Public Sector Reform Program (PSRP) has failed to effectively manage many of the more fundamental issues and problems facing the public service, such as low salary, corruption and poor delivery of public services" (Owusu 2005). Similarly, the senior minister in charge of PSRs has acknowledged the failure of earlier reforms and is currently looking for new reform strategies. As the minister put it rather candidly, "After five (5) years of reform and experimentation, the public services have not enhanced their ability to deliver services. They have not become more cost effective. And they have not become any more accountable to the public through changes in their methods or work than they were when we started on this reform process."[1]

Uganda

The Uganda Civil Service in the 1980s was in a state of crisis and disarray, which created the impetus for major reforms.[2] Uganda, like Ghana, is considered a relatively success case among Africa's public sector reformers. Part of this relative success is rooted in the National Resistance Movement (NRM) Government's desire and commitment to restore the country to normalcy and the road to economic development after many years of instability. According to the Adam Smith Institute of London (2002), Uganda has made remarkable progress at reducing poverty with the poverty headcount declining from 56 percent in 1992 to 44 percent in 1997 and more recently to less than 35 percent. Uganda's experience with regard to reducing poverty, according to this London think tank, is in concurrence with the more recent reviews regarding the importance that institutional arrangements play in determining policy outcomes. As the erstwhile IMF Managing Director, Michelle Camdessus, once remarked, "Few would dispute that sound social, political and economic institutions are necessary, if not sufficient conditions for the sustained implementation of sound macroeconomic policies" (Camdessus 1999). According to Uganda's Prime Minister and Minister for Public Service, "African civil servants and public administrators need to cope with the changing performance requirements brought about by globalisation and modernisation. They should share experiences and put in place strategies aimed at improved performance and service delivery through prompt policy coordination, monitoring, evaluation and feedback to stakeholders."[3] In the words of Professor Apollo Nsibambi, "the Uganda Public Service Reform Programme was designed to strengthen the public service to improve service delivery. The new phase of the Public Service Strategy will support measures that put in place service that focuses on and responds to the priorities of the government with the defined role of supporting a decentralisation policy and the growth of the private sector."[4]

Decentralization has been at the forefront of government's reform program. Since the coming to power in 1986 of the NRM Government, significant steps to decentralize power to local governments have been taken in an attempt to fulfill its Ten Point Program and to establish popular democracy in the country. Decentralization, according to the government, was not therefore "regarded merely as a policy goal that was intended to shift responsibility for development to local authorities, but as a policy instrument that would establish local democracy and improve accountability, efficiency, equity, effectiveness and sustainability in the provision of social services across the country" (Moses 2003).

Studies carried out in Uganda in the late 1990s indicate that the payroll in the public sector fell from 320,000 to 180,000.[5] Contrary to popular belief, large reductions have been achieved in Uganda with few compulsory redundancies that are in the region of 14,000. This is about 10 percent of the overall figure in Uganda.[6] Reductions in the Uganda civil service were achieved through various means including eliminating "ghost workers" and enforcing retirement ages. Also used was the purely cosmetic expedient of transferring civil servants to another agency such as an "enclave" revenue authority where they no longer counted as civil servants, though still paid out of the public purse.[7]

Uganda has, over the last two decades, taken radical steps to reduce numbers (by one-half), and pay levels have increased considerably in real terms. Currently, a comprehensive program is underway with continued efforts to improve organizational structures, introduce results-based management, new management information systems, and a divestiture program to set up autonomous agencies.[8] According to the mentioned report of the Donor Public Service Reform Working Groups, some of the critical factors that have contributed to the success of the CSR in Uganda include the following:

- Strong political support from the President
- Effective collaboration with a range of stakeholders
- Clarity of vision and defined strategy (government knew what it wanted)
- Winning over managers in the civil service earlier on (They supported reforms even though they faced difficult adjustments; for example, some ministries were abolished.)
- Early attention to capacity building in line with ability to undertake reforms

However, sustaining the early success of the program has been a challenge and hence the need to reexamine and redefine objectives and recurrent program. Furthermore, "the institutional features that appear to account for Uganda's initial success—strong political support to technocratic or bureaucratic elites with some degree of insulation from political and societal interests—also help explain why such reforms are susceptible to a process of unraveling" (Robinson 2006). Also, the main explanation for the loss of reform momentum (or even reversal of gains made) lies in the imperative of preserving the institutional foundations of neopatrimonial politics (Robinson 2006).

Besides, as pointed out by D. Kalinaki, Museveni's reform agenda has a mixed record on fighting corruption. It has passed laws, set up antigraft bodies, and appointed at least half a dozen commissions of inquiry to investigate claims. Apart from a few junior officials occasionally fed to the court system to appease the gallery, the government has failed to prosecute any significant officials implicated in corruption, even where such recommendations have been made.[9] The challenge of Uganda, therefore, has been in sustaining the momentum of reform. "Failure to sustain the momentum of governance reforms may have an adverse impact on wider achievements in relation to economic recovery, poverty reduction, and political stability as the political prerogatives of regime maintenance prevail over pragmatic developmental goals.[10]

Kenya

Kenya's CSR program is comparable to Tanzania's which arose primarily from the need to reduce overstaffing and address low pay and also improve service delivery performance.[11] At its inception, the CSR program was to be implemented in two phases. The first phase comprised the reduction of numbers of civil servants through the Voluntary Early Retirement Scheme (VERS) and a ministerial rationalization pilot scheme in twelve key ministries. This pilot scheme, if successful, was to be replicated throughout the rest of the remaining ministries during the second phase.

The ministerial rationalization pilot scheme relied heavily on outside consultants, mainly from the university and think tanks. They were brought in because the government thought they would be impartial and, hence, come up with the most appropriate government structures for implementation. In this process, the government overlooked one fundamental issue on the nature of organizations. These outside consultants did not know the internal organizational politics going on in the ministries they were assigned to restructure. The result was that, after the consultants had made their reports and were paid for work done, the reports were rejected wholesale by the civil servants who were supposed to implement them.

The official argument was that these civil servants could not implement reports that did not reflect their ideas and opinions. In other words, the consultants' reports lacked ownership within the civil service. The real problem, however, was not wholly with the consultants. It can be said to be systemic, and some answers can be found in the study conducted in Kenya, cited by Blunt and Jones (1992, 9), which stated "one factor which emerged in the study as essential to managerial success was the building and maintenance of political connections. This consisted not in building an independent political base, but in gaining regular access to top politicians in order to influence policy decisions, supply of resources, and protection against politicization and inappropriate policies. Such political support has to be earned through loyalty and network building." With such a system in place, many top civil servants have always managed to thwart efforts that introduce changes they perceive as not favoring them.

During the evaluation of the ministerial rationalization carried out during Phase I of the reforms, it was not, therefore, surprising that the same government that sanctioned the consultancies and the program found out it had all manner of faults. The government noted the following short comings, among many others: the approach was slow and took long to yield results; it led to uncoordinated and fragmented rationalization, and the program was perceived to be centrally driven by the Directorate of Personnel Management (Government of Kenya 1999).

Whichever way one looks at Phase I of the civil service reforms in Kenya, it had its shortcomings. The WB, in its project document for the financing of Phase II of the reforms noted that "the civil service reforms program implemented between 1993 and 1998 focused essentially on staff and wage bill reduction. A significant reduction in staff size was achieved through a number of reduction measures including the VERS. Very little attention was paid to the performance enhancing components of the reform programme: pay reform, personnel management and training, and finance management" (WB 2000, 4).

Having learned its lessons in the first phase, the ministerial rationalization was pushed to the second phase, and civil servants took full control of the process. The components not achieved in first phase were also earmarked for implementation in the second phase. Although civil servants were to be fully in charge of Phase II, the beginning of this phase, upon donor pressure, saw the introduction of "private sector technocrats" to head key ministries of finance and agriculture and also, along with them, came the head of the public service and secretary to the cabinet. Although the new appointments were all filled by indigenous Kenyans, it was expected and typical of the key principles of New Public Management that they would infuse private sector management techniques in a bid to reverse declining economic growth, among other things.

The new appointments were received with mixed feelings in different quarters of the civil service. They were given various labels, from "technocrats" to "dream team." This team, to say the least, did not receive the entire support it needed to turn the economy around. "In certain quarters in the civil service, there is a view that within the high echelons of the government, especially among the ministers, lurked growing impatience with what was perceived as airs affected by permanent secretaries. This resentment built up in the reshuffle of 1999 that brought in Dr. Richard Leakey (head of public service and secretary to the cabinet) and his team"

(Warigi 2000, 10). The commentary further noted "this high level discomfort has further been fed by the media and donor adulations of Dr. Leakey's so called Dream Team. Donor assumptions that these technocrats would turn around the country and do what politicians have failed to do have done little to boost the politician's self-confidence. And you can trust politicos with ear to the President [*sic*] have been fighting back, through palace intrigues" (Warigi 2000, 10).

The beginning of Phase II, apart from the infusion of "technocrats," also saw a change of tactics in the reform process. Whereas in Phase I, consultants were the lead group and civil servants only worked alongside them, in Phase II, the civil servants were in the lead and could only invite in any consultants as and when they felt a need. Even so, the first priority was given to civil servants who could provide similar services, before turning to the outside. The Ministerial Civil Service Committees were, therefore, wholly responsible through their respective permanent secretaries for all the changes proposed in the ministries and their subsequent implementation. This phase also saw the integration of CSRs together with the financial reforms taking place at the same time. The Medium Term Expenditure Framework (MTEF) implemented by the Ministry of Finance sought to provide a link between policy, planning, and budgeting by requiring ministries to concentrate public resources on delivery of core services, implementation of high-priority physical infrastructure projects, and budget allocation based more on output performance than input controls. The two initiatives, running concurrently, led to the two committees being merged into one after the realization that the MTEF exercise integrated the financial and budgetary aspect into ministerial rationalization initiatives of the CSR.

There has been considerable progress in the implementation of CSRs in Kenya in recent times. In September 2006, the government of Kenya "officially launched a key plank in the public service reform strategy." The strategy, dubbed the Rapid Results Initiative, aims at reducing corruption, enhancing efficiency and accountability and introducing performance measures. After many years of poor governance and economic mismanagement under the Moi regime, Kenya's new government of National Rainbow Coalition party (NARC) was eager to deliver on its electoral promise and quickly reverse Kenya's falling socioeconomic indicators and achieve tangible results within a short period of time. In January 2004, during a capacity enhancement mission, senior government officials and leaders of the private sector in Kenya emphasized that "the key capacity enhancement challenge in Kenya is the implementation of government's comprehensive and ambitious Economic Recovery Strategy (ERS) for Wealth and Employment Creation."[12] Although the government was fully committed to the policies outlined in the ERS, there was an acute need for assisting the government in achieving tangible results that would meet the high expectations of the general public. The Rapid Results Approach (RRA) was deemed by government to be an important and timely tool that would help in jump-starting the change processes so desperately needed in turning around the public sector. In this regard, the WB team conducted a number of workshops with senior government officials from eighteen ministries.

More than two hundred government officials were introduced to the Rapid Results Approach (RRA), and others were trained to become Rapid Results coaches, who would champion the results orientation in government operations. Furthermore, the team helped the government prioritize its investment program and strengthened its results orientation. Many of Kenya's current leaders see the RRA as an important implementation tool, which will speed up reform and generate tangible results quickly. However, as observed in the *Nation* newspaper, "with the public service, it is not just about putting in place the required systems and measures; it is about radically transforming a massive bureaucracy with an entrenched culture and mindset that might be resistant to change, having known no other way of doing things."[13]

President Mwai Kibaki has also emphasized the importance of the CSRs that have been initiated. While addressing the monthly American Chamber of Commerce luncheon in Nairobi in September 2006, he indicated that his government had "embarked on an ambitious public service reforms programme, which includes the introduction of results-based management, performance contracts and service charters in the civil service, local government and parastatals."[14] What seems to have affected the momentum of Kenya's reform agenda is the postelection violence that disrupted the civil service performance as well as the economy whose current growth rate has dropped from an estimated 7 percent during the pre-election period to nearly 3 percent in the first quarter of 2008. Nearly 350,000 people were displaced, and according to the *Independent*, the tourism industry, which was Kenya's biggest foreign exchange earner with annual revenue of US$1, was described earlier this year as "dead" by the Kenyan Association of Tour Operators.[15]

Kenya in the Postconflict Era

Kenyan President Kibaki and opposition leader Raila Odinga in February 2008 signed an agreement to end the country's postelection crisis. At a ceremony in Nairobi, the two men put their signatures to a power-sharing deal brokered by the former United Nations Secretary-General Kofi Annan. A coalition government, comprising members of the current ruling party, Party for National Unity, and the opposition, was formed.

Some 1,500 people died in political violence after Odinga said he was robbed of victory in December's polls. International observers agreed that December's election count was flawed.

The postelection violence saw thousands of people targeted because they belonged to ethnic groups seen as either pro-government or pro-opposition. Although the level of violence had fallen by early January, there were concerns that a failure to reach a deal would lead to a fresh round of bloodletting. Negotiations between the government and opposition lasted more than a month, stalling several times.

Portfolios Shared

The new coalition is headed by President Kibaki, and Odinga—whose Orange Democratic Movement (ODM) is the largest in parliament—took the newly created post of prime minister. Each party will nominate a deputy prime minister, with other ministerial portfolios being divided equally between the two parties. After the deal was reached, Annan said, "Compromise was necessary for the survival of this country." He urged all Kenyans to support the agreement, saying, "The job of national reconciliation and national reconstruction is not for the leaders alone. It must be carried out in every neighbourhood, village, hamlet of the nation."

"New Chapter"

Speaking after the signing, Kibaki said, "This process has reminded us that as a nation there are more issues that unite than that divide us. . . . We've been reminded we must do all in our power to safeguard the peace that is the foundation of our national unity. . . . Kenya has room for all of us."

Mr. Odinga said, "With the signing of this agreement, we have opened a new chapter in our country's history—from the era or phase of confrontation to the beginning of cooperation. We, on our side, are completely committed to ensuring that this agreement will succeed."

Both men thanked those who had stood by Kenya in what Odinga called its "hour of need," including Annan, the African Union, the European Union, the United States, and the United Nations. They also urged Kenyans to move forward together without ethnic divisions.

After eight weeks of uncertainty in the political atmosphere as well as peace, there is somehow a glimpse of hope and light to the beautiful land of Kenya.

Tom Casey, a spokesman for the U.S. State Department, said the agreement was "an important and very positive step forward." He added, "It allows the Kenyan people to move forward with a very basic issue of governance."

British Prime Minister Gordon Brown welcomed the new power-sharing agreement: "Kenya's leaders have reached a power-sharing agreement that represents a triumph for peace and diplomacy, and a renunciation of the violence that has scarred a country of such enormous potential," he said.

In western Kenya, the scene of the some of the worst violence, there was some skepticism about the agreement. Paul Waweru, 56, who fled his home and is now living in a camp in Eldoret, said, "The deal between Raila and Kibaki will help to cool down the situation, but I doubt if it will enable us to get back to our homes."

But in Nairobi's Kibera slum, there were celebrations. "The general mood among people is that of happiness," said Nelson Ochieng. "We are tired of the political crisis. I was a barber but my shop was burnt. Now I'm jobless, and the end of this crisis means that I can rebuild my business."

Kenya Swears in Historical Coalition Government

Kenya, in April 2008, swore in a power-sharing government to end a bloody postelection crisis, which claimed at least 1,500 lives, with new Prime Minister Odinga vowing to bring power to the people.

Odinga, 63, was sworn in as prime minister before his rival, President Kibaki, 76, as well as former U.N. Chief Annan, who brokered the power-sharing accord.

Also present during the swearing in ceremony in Nairobi were Ugandan President Yoweri Museveni, former Kenyan President Daniel Arap Moi, and representatives from neighboring states. "We have been to hell and back. We must preserve the sanctity of our nation and remain united, but our unity cannot be based on words and goodwill alone," Odinga said. "Kenya will have no longer a ruling class. The rulers are the people. Power will forever be with the people of Kenya. Fellow Kenyans, I give you myself in your service."

A handful of people from Kibaki's dominant Kikuyu and Moi's Kalenjin tribes had controlled Kenya's economy since independence from Britain in 1963, leaving the majority living in poverty. "It's one government of two equal partners. I'm determined to provide decisive leadership and to help build democratic institutions," said Odinga, who had launched three failed attempts to become president. Odinga vowed to broaden reforms to ensure equal distribution of land, jobs, and national wealth among the country's forty-plus tribes.

Kibaki said he would monitor the performance of ministers in the country, where growth projections for this year were slashed from 7 percent to between 4.5 and 6 percent. He stated, "I want to emphasise that you will be expected to show results and excel in your portfolios. Kenyans will be monitoring your performance and will be judging you by the quality and timeliness of services."

The new government is made up of ninety-three ministers and assistant ministers, sparking complaints that it is too big for a nation where 60 percent of the people earn less than a dollar a day. Annan urged Kenyans to support the government, saying the deeply divided country had a long way to go after the crisis that ruined its reputation as a beacon of stability in a region beset by conflict. "We have an opportunity to put Kenya back on track and build a stronger Kenya," he said. "It is essential that you all support the leaders and the government . . . You are on an important journey. Stay the course, work with them, support them, and don't believe that now you've got a government, all is resolved and we can relax." Annan later added, "Peace is precious. Let's not lose it once again."

Kenyan civil society groups have lamented that several ministries in the new cabinet overlap, chiefly citing the Ministry of Public Health and Sanitation with that of medical services. Others include livestock, fisheries, and agriculture that had been under the same docket but are now separate. Roads were separated from public works, and industrialization created from trade. Environment and mineral resources were separated from forestry and wildlife. But Odinga defended the size, saying, "It is not the size of the wave, but the motion of the sea that moves the ship. Don't look at the size of this cabinet, look at its products."

The swearing-in ceremony, held on Thursday, April 17, 2008, at State House Nairobi, was overshadowed by the killing of at least twenty people, mainly in the capital, Rift Valley, and Central provinces, in an ongoing police crackdown on the politically linked Mungiki sect since Monday, April 14, 2008. The sect, which has become a violent criminal network, has previously accused the police of beheading its jailed leader's wife, Virginia Nyako, wife of Maina Njenga. Odinga, however, welcomed the sect for talks: "We want to sit down with Mungiki to talk as Kenyans. They should stop fighting and killing people," Odinga said.

Malawi

Malawi's postindependence government of Kamuzu Banda adopted the option of an open, market friendly economy at a time when many African countries were having command economies.[16] Both GDP and per capita income grew in the 1960s and 1970s. However, this state of affairs changed drastically in the early 1980s due to a series of shocks, including deterioration of terms of trade, oil crises, disruption along the external transport routes through Mozambique due to the prevailing insecurity caused by civil war, and periodic droughts (Adamolekun 2002, 275). Like other sub-Saharan African countries examined, Malawi did implement reforms in the civil service in the 1990s and early 2000s. From the perspective of the WB, the "composition of the Malawi civil service was seriously skewed" (Danielson 2001). Lower grade workers such as watchmen, cleaners, workmen, messengers, and other subordinate staff were overstaffed, whereas senior positions often remained vacant due to lack of suitable staff. Moreover, "the exact number of junior civil servants in the industrial class (IC) and the subordinate class (SC) was unknown since the recruitment of the lowest grades was the responsibility of individual departments that used this authority to hire large numbers of clients.[17] The remedy to this anomaly, as it was done elsewhere in sub-Saharan Africa, was to establish the exact number of employees in the IC and the SC, reduce staff numbers in these grades through a retrenchment program, improve personnel and payroll management, and create more favorable salary structures for the highly qualified professionals in senior positions (WB 1993, 1994).

The WB's approach to the Malawi reforms was to use the "enclave approach," which singled out government departments and agencies that were expected to operate as centers from where the reforms would spread throughout the entire civil service. This, however, brought a conflict between the "enclave" agencies, thus promoting reform with active support of the WB against top officials of the "traditional" ministries, many of them left over from the previous Banda regime (Adamolekun 1997, 215–17).

Origin of Malawi's Reform Program

After independence in 1964, Malawi's "political stability" was largely achieved at the expense of individual freedoms. Basic human rights and democratic principles were trampled on, and a highly centralized system of political and economic authority was instituted with the aim of controlling instead of empowering Malawians for sustainable human development.[18]

In 1985, the Herbecq Review Commission was set up with the primary mandate of assessing modifications needed in staff structure, career development, and grading in addition to personnel management so as to make best use of the human and financial resources available. In addition, the capacity of Malawi's educational and training institutions to provide for the needs of the public corporations and the civil service was undermined. This review was carried out when Malawi was implementing a medium-term stabilization program jointly with the WB and the IMF, covering the period of 1981 to 1982 and 1985 to 1986. The program was aimed at making the deficit more manageable, particularly using expenditure restraint to reduce the budget deficit. By 1987, the core civil service had grown to 50,008 as compared to 10,745 in 1964.

More recent reform initiatives have arisen from national political developments. In March 1993, Malawians decided to go for a multiparty system of government through a referendum. The new government issued a "policy statement on civil service reform and institutional development" in May 1994. The policy states in part that "government recognises the critical role that the civil service plays in its effort to realise national development objectives. As the operational arm of government, the civil service is charged with the task of providing an enabling physical, economic and administrative environment that facilitates the achievement of the nation's social and economic objectives. To this end, it is government's policy to periodically subject public sector organisations, including the civil service parastatal agencies and local government institutions to external reviews of their operations, responsibilities, functions, structures and establishment levels" (Banda 1996). Also in the same year, " . . . the government promulgated a Public Service Act that provides for clarification of the role the civil service, equal access to public employment, merit-based recruitment and promotion, and increased predictability, accountability and transparency in the policies and practices of the public service."[19]

The comprehensive PSR program is now in the context of the country's Vision 2020 statement and the need for national capacity building to translate the vision into social, economic, and political deliverables. The country's Vision 2020 states, inter alia, "By the year 2020, Malawi as a God fearing nation will be secure, ecologically balanced, democratically mature, environmentally sustainable, self reliant with equal opportunities for and active participation by all, having social services, vibrant cultural and religious values and being a technologically driven middle-income country."[20] And according to Banda (1996), public service sector is one of the "conditiones sine qua non" that will enable the country to realize her vision.

The public sector reforms in Malawi, like in many other African countries, face the problem of prioritizing and sequencing the key implementation measures. Despite having adopted a comprehensive approach to PSR, Malawi's reform program is still faced with serious challenges. These challenges include the failure to develop a public sector that is visionary as well as mission-oriented and has the ability to effectively deliver quality services and address problems that confront the people. Then, there is the challenge of creating a public sector institutional capacity to promote sustainable human development through participatory approaches to the formulation, implementation, monitoring, and evaluation of socioeconomic development programs.

Finally, there is the problem of building consensual PSR strategies to tackle socioeconomic development irrespective of differences in political party ideologies. A successful implementation of public sector reforms in

Malawi will require a transformational and mission-driven leadership and a broad national commitment to the reform process.[21]

The case of Malawi CSR cannot be said to be a success story. In the words of a senior economist, Malawi has been considered to be "a kind of invalid, which needs a long period of rehabilitation before it will be back on its feet again. We cannot even begin to think in terms of sustainable development. Malawi itself is unsustainable. In the meantime, we need to keep the invalid going with massive safety net programmes" (Devereux 2000). Despite the foregoing observation, owing to the enormity and political sensitivity of the reform program and the severe limitations on capacity to manage reform, "such a framework will take ten to twenty years to fully implement in most countries. Civil service reform is an art, not a science. Committed reformers within the concerned government know best what they need and how to get there" (Wescott 1999, 1).

French-Speaking West African Public Sector Reforms

Danielson (2001) has analyzed economic and institutional reforms in French-speaking West African countries in the context of institutional and economic reforms. According to Danielson (2001), economic performance, measured by growth of per capita incomes, has not been encouraging, despite far-reaching reforms, including privatization, liberalization, and deep regional integration (Danielson 2001, 1). Furthermore, social indicators suggest that poverty reduction has not been achieved through reforms. This is corroborated by the fact that indicators of access to primary health care, inputs, and outcomes in primary education show deteriorating trends in the majority of these countries (Danielson 2001, 1).

The potential for reforms in countries belonging to the West African Economic and Monetary Union (WAEMA) differ somewhat from those in other parts of sub-Saharan Africa (Kayizzi-Mugerwa 2003, 106). The institutional nature of the WAEMA, which includes a central bank, limits the extent to which individual countries can exercise monetary policy. The region has thus experienced relatively low levels of inflation. This not withstanding, the fact that several WAEMA members are among countries that receive most foreign aid per capita in the world, poor public finances are likely to reduce social service delivery.[22]

Reforms in the WAEMA countries are characterised by two common themes. In most cases, a rapidly deteriorating economic situation, political turmoil, or growing social unrest forced the governments radically to change economic policy in the 1980s. For example, natural protests against perceived corruption, followed by social unrest, forced the government of Benin to resign and the successors to dismantle large parts of the bureaucracy.[23]

Cote d'Ivoire

In Cote d'Ivoire, a mounting debt crisis forced the government to accede to reforms. Cote d'Ivoire (Ivory Coast) was once West Africa's economic success story in the early 1990s. It is a country where people looked for economic opportunities from the entire French West African region. But it has been a very different story since 1999 (Zuckerman 2006). In December 1999, a military coup, the first ever in Cote d'Ivoire's history, overthrew the government. Junta leader Robert Guei is believed to have massively rigged the elections that were held in late December 2000 and declared himself the winner.[24] Popular protest forced him to step aside and brought runner-up Laurent Gbagbo into power. Ivorian dissidents and disaffected members of the military launched a failed coup attempt in September 2002. Rebel forces claimed the Northern half of the country, and in January 2003 were granted ministerial posts in government of national unity under the auspices of the Linas-Marcoussis Peace Accord. President Gbagbo and rebel forces resumed implementation of the peace accord in December 2003 after a three month stalemate, but issues that sparked the civil war such as land reform and grounds for citizenship, remained unresolved.

On March 4, 2007, after weeks of closed-door negotiations led by the president of Burkina Faso, Blaise Compaore, in Ouagadougou, President Gbagbo, and New Forces leader Guillaume Soro, who was named prime minister, announced they had agreed to a peace agreement aimed at reunifying the country and holding new elections.[25] The Ouagadougou Accord foresaw a new transitional government and relaunch of the stalled voter registration and identification process to enable elections to be held within ten months. As of May 2007, government ministers, particularly health, education, finance, and interior officials, gradually returned to their posts in the northern part of the country.[26]

Mali

In Mali, a deteriorating economic situation created a political crisis, and the transition government widened and deepened the earlier reforms to correct the structural imbalances of the mid-1980s. In most countries in the region, agreements with the IMF were typically seen as a last resort (Kayizzi-Mugerwa 2003, 108). In Burkina Faso, for instance, where the policy of rectification had been going on since 1987, the 1991 IMF agreement broadly endorsed that policy.[27]

In contrast, Senegal's performance under the homegrown reform program was weak, and the 1985 IMF agreement introduced new components, including the amendment of the labor code, dismantling of public monopolies, and reorganization of the system of revenue collection.[28] In several cases, the French West African region has tended to associate reforms with a harsh economic environment.[29] Relations with the IMF have been uneasy, with programs subject to reversal.

Several countries within the WAEMA have taken important steps toward reforming the civil service. Staffing levels have been reduced, and the wage bill has been cut.[30] The state of CSRs between the WAEMA members differs substantially. Some countries, such as Senegal, have been able to introduce a system of promotion based on merit and seniority and to link this to indicators of service delivery. Other countries, for instance, Niger, failed to come to terms with their expanding but relatively inefficient bureaucracies (Lienert and Modi 1997). Nevertheless, to reduce public employment, the said countries have used a number of approaches including the removal of employment guarantees to new graduates in countries such as Benin, Cote d'Ivoire, and Niger, while compulsory retirement or reduction in the statutory retirement age has been introduced in Burkina Faso and Senegal.[31]

In the WAEMA member states, like elsewhere in sub-Saharan Africa, the results of the reform program in the public sector have not had substantial impact on poverty reduction. While many of these countries have managed "to reduce the size of their workforce, incentive systems and pay structures still leave a lot to be desired" (Danielson 2001, 22).

Benin

Benin is the larger of the two, small irregular land strips between Nigeria in the east and Ghana in the west on the Gulf of Guinea of the Atlantic Ocean (Adamolekun 2002, 177). This country was originally the prominent West African kingdom of Dahomey that arose in the fifteenth century.[32] The territory became a French colony in 1872 and attained independence on August 1, 1960, as the Republic of Benin. A succession of military governments ended in 1972 with the rise to power of Mathieu Kerekou, who established a government based on Marxist-Leninist principles. Kerekou's government could not meet the state payroll or even obtain external credits; he was abandoned by his former clientele and faced rising street protests as well as a barrage of denunciations from intellectuals, teachers, civil servants, unions, and students (Lewis 1998, 346). Kerekou, isolated, could not resist seizure of power by "civil society" (Lewis 1998, 347). A move to representative government began in 1989, and two years later, free elections ushered in Nicephore Soglo, former prime minister, as president, marking the first successful transfer of power in Africa from a dictatorship to a democracy. Kerekou was returned to power in the elections held in 1996 and 2001, though some irregularities were alleged (Lewis 1998, 347).

Benin's economy remains largely underdeveloped and dependent on subsistence agriculture, cotton production, and regional trade. Growth in real output has averaged around 5 percent in the past six years, but rapid population growth has offset much of this increase. Inflation has subsided over the past several years. Reforms to the land tenure system, the commercial justice system, and the financial sector were included in Benin's US$307 million Millennium Challenge Account grant signed in February 2006.[33] The 2001 privatization policy continues in telecommunications, water, electricity, and agriculture in spite of government reluctance. The Paris Club and bilateral creditors have eased the external debt situation, with Benin benefiting from a G8 debt reduction announced in July 2005, while pressing for more rapid structural reforms.

Genesis of Benin's Reform Program

Improving the performance of public administration system in Benin emerged as a major issue in the late 1980s when the government embarked on the implementation of the structural adjustment program.[34] However, the problem of cost containment (reducing staff strength and the payroll), because of serious fiscal deficits, predominated. The issues of cost containment and of performance improvement were both raised at the National Conference in 1990 where it was agreed that a national forum of public organizations would be held to undertake a review of the problems and to propose remedial measures (Mostafa 2002, 182). What happened in Benin seems to have inspired other French West African people to hold their governments to account. This is what Crawford Young calls "the beauty of something unique, incomparable."

Conclusion

In examining public sector reform programs across the African continent, one has to bear in mind that "the one-size-fits-it-all solution cannot work since it fails to take into consideration each country's peculiar conditions and circumstances. Furthermore, by not taking into consideration individual countries' differences in performance, or even acknowledging the possibility of good and poor performers within countries, the policies tended to ignore any potentially valuable lessons that could have been learned from the performance of public-sector organizations.

The failure of the reforms has demonstrated the need for a different approach to the reform agenda. There is need, for instance, to use a flexible approach to accommodate country-specific constraints and challenges facing organizations. There is also the question of the ability to adapt to constraints where the performance of public organizations has been greatly influenced by a series of external challenges, including the colonial legacies (Ekeh 1975; Alemika 1993). The wider culture in which the organizations are immersed (Dia 1994), the use of organizations as tools of popular patronage as opposed to being a mechanism for providing public goods (Sandbrook and Oelbaum 1999), and the changing livelihood of employees in response to economic crisis and reforms is a phenomenon that has greatly affected public organizations in Africa (Owusu 2001; 2005).

In general, Levy has argued that Tanzania has been a promising and innovative performer in East Africa and, indeed, the wider sub-Saharan Africa. Levy (2003), argues that in Africa, despite setbacks, and this may come as a surprise, formal rules and regulations in public service still exist, but more attention needs to be paid to the political dimensions in each setting.

It should be noted that in many sub-Saharan African countries, pressures on government functions during the last decade also encouraged the development of important innovations such as performance contracts, contracting out of essential public services, and a variety of joint public sector-private sector ventures. Moreover, "in the wake of privatization, many governments began to develop regulatory mechanisms to ensure that national goals and standards were respected by the new private owners" (Grindle 1991). In a study by the United Nations Research Institute for Social Development (UNRISD), an analysis is made of the impact of public sector reform in eight countries. The analysis highlights the importance of the political dynamics behind them. Special attention is given to donor involvement and concerns over efficiency as well as accountability are identified (Therkildsen 2002).

There is no doubt "that great strides are being made in the majority of sub-Saharan African countries toward improving the quality of governance through institutional reforms aimed at enhancing accountability and transparency. These pressures are not likely to abate" (Adamolekun 2002, 156).

It may be too early to comprehensively assess the outcomes of the reforms carried out in many of the African countries; nonetheless, it must be borne in mind that the reforms depend as much on political factors as on managerial arrangements. Support for the reforms remains largely mixed, as can be expected with reforms that result in mixed, uncertain, or distributed benefits.

Finally, it is important to recognize that "most countries do not have the institutional capacity to manage and coordinate the entire reform effort, communicate with the various domestic and international stakeholders, contain corruption, reduce cost and size, alleviate poverty, while at the same time creating an enabling environment for globalization and private sector investment and development" (Kiggundu 1997, 158).

The challenges offered by public sector reforms in sub-Saharan Africa have had far-reaching consequences for the countries of this vast region. Although countries found in this region reflect great variety in their territories, populations, cultures, resources, and historical legacies, the diversity of this region should not obscure the common problems and challenges evident during the last five decades of post independence development. Africans have embraced reforms with varying degrees of success, yet the region as a whole has experienced some of the most formidable, if not intractable, problems in the recent history of the developing world.

3

Rwanda's Public Sector Reform Program After the 1994 War and Genocide

> In Rwanda today there are millions of people who still ask why the United Nations Mission for Rwanda (UNAMIR), the United Nations (UN) and the international community allowed this disaster to happen. I do not have all the answers or even most of them.
>
> —*Lt. Gen. Romeo Dallaire,* Shake Hands with the Devil: The Failure of Humanity in Rwanda

Rwanda was engulfed in a debilitating genocide in 1994 that witnessed unprecedented loss of life and destruction of property. It was the purest genocide since 1945 and perhaps the single, greatest act of evil since Pol Pot turned Cambodia into a killing field.[1] The numbers, estimated by the United Nations Organization, that were killed by the end of June 1994 were as high as one million. By the end of July, it is estimated that more than one million lives had been lost. What happened in Rwanda in 1994 is perhaps best captured in the words of Lt. Gen. Romeo Dallaire (2003, xvii), commander of the United Nations peace-keeping force in Rwanda, who described it as a story of "betrayal, failure, naïveté, indifference, hatred, genocide, war, inhumanity and evil." So in July 1994, when the Government of National Unity took over the reigns of power in Rwanda, "the air was filled with the stench of death; heaps of corpses were on every inch of land while others floated freely on lakes and rivers" (Smith 2004, 101). In other words, Rwanda was on its deathbed after the genocide.

The genocide of 1994 resulted in the destruction of the country's social fabric, its human resource base, institutional capacity, and economic and social infrastructure. Rwanda's economic activity, according to the IMF in its "Enhanced Structural Adjustment Facility, Economic and Financial

Policy Framework Paper for 1998/99–2000/01," declined by about 50 percent.[2] In the United Nations secretary-general's report, the United Nations pledged to strengthen the coordination of humanitarian and disaster relief assistance to Rwanda "for a solution to the problem of refugees, the restoration of total peace, reconstruction and socio-economic development."[3]

Other efforts at post genocide reconstruction came from the WB Emergency Recovery Program, which grew out of two donor meetings held in Paris in September and October 1994, which were among the first major initiatives specifically aimed at reconstruction of the country. This program was designated to "help the new government begin the restoration of key economic and social services, rebuild the institutional capacity necessary for sustainable economic recovery, and design a coherent economic policy framework that would provide the private sector with the means to resume operations and create jobs."[4] Other key development partners include the United Kingdom, which signed a Memorandum of Understanding (MOU) in October 1999 in which the Department for International Development (DFID) committed itself to a long-term engagement in Rwanda aimed at helping the country meet international development targets. The aim of the DFID program in Rwanda is to support mutually agreed MOU objectives on peace, reconciliation, poverty alleviation, economic reform, and open, accountable government. The DFID has, among other support, provided technical assistance to the GOR's Poverty Reduction Strategy Process, Medium-Term Expenditure Framework (MTEF), RRA, CSR, capacity building, and reform of the education sector as well as providing support to the demobilization of ex-combatants.[5] Currently, the United Kingdom government provides a total of £46 million annually in development assistance to Rwanda, according to a release from the DFID office in Kigali.[6]

The government of Rwanda, through Vision 2020, has put in place a policy framework that is expected to transform the country from an agriculture-based economy to an information-rich, knowledge-based society and economy within the next twenty years. This is largely through the GOR's recognition of the role that ICTs can play in accelerating the socio-economic development of the country toward an information and knowledge economy.[7] One of the key objectives of Rwanda's Vision 2020 is to turn the country into an ICT center of excellence in the region.

Since 1995, Rwanda has made remarkable recovery and considerable progress on various socioeconomic and political fronts. The average GDP growth rate between 1995 and 2004 was about 8 percent per annum. The genesis of this recovery was laid when, in 1997, the government of Rwanda adopted a transition program to consolidate the fragile socioeconomic recovery attained during 1995 and 1996 and laid the basis for national reconstruction, sustainable growth, participatory decision making, and poverty reduction. A new constitution was promulgated in May 2003, followed by multiparty parliamentary and presidential elections, which were successfully conducted in August and September 2003. These were the first democratic elections to be held since the country's independence from Belgium, on July 1, 1962. Besides this, Rwanda signed an MOU with the African Peer Review Mechanism on March 9, 2003, in which she committed herself to "provide all necessary resources to facilitate the processes involved at the national level, access to all the required information and stakeholders."

Despite this remarkable recovery and improved international standing, Rwanda remains highly dependent on foreign aid. According to the Organization of European Economic Development (OECD), foreign aid, between 2000 and 2004, accounted for about 50 percent of the current budget and 80 percent of the development budget, even though the share of government revenues to GDP has recently increased. A recent review of Rwanda's Poverty Reduction and Growth Facility (PRGF) by the IMF acknowledges that "Rwanda's economic performance strengthened in 2005. Driven by a recovery in agriculture, growth rebounded to 6% and inflation fell. Macroeconomic policy implementation was broadly on track. On the structural side, progress was mixed, partly due to capacity constraints. In particular, reforms in public expenditure management remain pending."[8]

This chapter examines the various attempts by government, in collaboration with multilateral and bilateral partners, to accelerate the country's growth and development as encapsulated in Vision 2020, Rwanda's blueprint for development. The chapter further examines, besides the various institutions and mechanisms established, the challenges encountered in the process of introducing reforms and their effects on the country's economy. At the heart of the country's continued stability lies the imperative to sustain the momentum of unity and reconciliation,[9] the fulcrum upon which future development will hinge.

Rwanda's Reform Agenda

Rwanda's reform agenda aims at tackling obstacles to growth. A continued focus on building capacity of both the civil service and the private sector is needed. "More specifically, reducing the cost of doing business will be key to stimulating private sector development."[10] These efforts have mainly concentrated on the rehabilitation and reconstruction of a shattered economy and infrastructure and the country's public sector, which were seriously affected by the events of 1994. Among the areas examined in this chapter is a fiscal and financial decentralization program that consists

Figure 3.1 Traditional residence of the Rwandan king in Nyanza, Southern Province of Rwanda.

of the devolution of decision-making powers to subnational governments that will allow mobilization of resources for implementation of government policy. Today, Rwanda is divided into five administrative provinces, with the city of Kigali as an autonomous province. Originally, there were twelve provinces. This radical restructuring of Rwanda's administration demonstrates the policy makers' desire to transform the country into a viable economy.

Rwanda's progress in her structural transformation has remained slow, as a stagnating manufacturing sector (as a share of GDP) indicates. Not much progress has been made in increasing exports, which, combined with continuously high debt financing, implies a worsening of the country's external debt sustainability (African Economic Outlook 2004–2005). While the poverty rate increased sharply from 47.5 percent in 1990 to 78 percent in 1994, it has declined steadily since then, reaching about 60 percent in 2000 and about 56 percent in 2005 (African Economic Outlook 2004–2005). Considerable progress has been made in the field of health and education. An accelerated immunization program has been implemented throughout the country, and rehabilitation of health facilities has been done in most parts of the country.

There has been a sharp increase in primary school enrollment ratios over the last few years, and Rwanda, according to a report by OECD (African Economic Outlook 2004–2005), could reach universal enrollment by

2010. The proportion of girls in primary schools is on a par with that of boys. Rwanda, which was among the poorest countries in human development index (HDI) during the late 1990s, ranked 159 out of 177 countries in the Human Development Report (2004).[11] Rwanda has been identified as a potential candidate for the Millennium Development Goals (MDGs) fast-tracking, which, if realized, would give the country a considerable boost in poverty reduction and growth (Human Development Report 2004).

Political and Socioeconomic Background

During the colonial and postcolonial periods, the government of Rwanda was characterised by a highly centralized state (MINALOC 2005). Decision-making and resource allocation were tightly maintained by the central government allowing it domination over political, social, and economic life. Accountability of the public sector was toward the center rather than to the citizens and communities. No wonder, therefore, that this highly centralized system of governance caused considerable inefficiencies in service delivery and consequently created a passive attitude regarding civic responsibilities among citizens (MINALOC 2005).

Earlier during the colonial period, the Belgian colonial administration "chose to create artificial divisions among Rwandans that reflected their own bitter divisions in their country, and that would obviously facilitate

Figure 3.2 Rwanda's Tourism and National Parks stand at the Berlin International Tourism exhibition (2007), in which Rwanda was declared the best exhibitor.

colonial exploitation and subjugation."[12] Successive postcolonial governments promoted an ideology that entrenched differences, created institutions that marginalized and discriminated against one section of Rwandan society, the Batutsi, and rewarded injustices and human rights abuses committed against them.

The divisionism encouraged and sponsored by the postcolonial leadership was exacerbated by impoverishment in the context of the prevailing global economic environment the country was operating in. As Woodward (1996) illustrates this further resentment, indeed desperation, arising from mass impoverishment would have been expected to arise in the Rwanda of the 1980s and early 1990s, even if inequality had not been worsening. A principal problem according to Woodward lay in the evolution of global commodity markets. For instance, between 1985 and 1992, the real world price of coffee, Rwanda's main export, fell by 72 percent, between 1986 and 1992, the real purchasing power of Rwanda's export earnings fell by 59 percent. The ensuing crisis in the state finances was a major reason for the adoption of a WB/IMF-sponsored structural adjustment program in late 1990, which itself contributed to social tensions and fears (Storey 1999a).

This very severe foreign exchange problem arose in the context of an agricultural sector already structurally crisis-ridden by a chronic shortage of land and rapid population growth, with associated declines in soil fertility, reflecting the exhaustion of an agricultural development model that placed little onus on intensification, innovation, or export-oriented production (Ulvin 1998, 57). More than half of all Rwandan farmers occupied farms of less than one hectare, often on ecologically fragile soils, while up to 25 percent of the population was landless (Mullen 1995, 23). In the most densely populated regions, this had the effect of postponing or ruling out marriage, because custom dictated that a man without sufficient land could not marry (Human Rights Watch 1999, 46). Surveys conducted in 1990 and 1992, in regions relatively unaffected by the war, found that 75 percent of the population had been watching their monetary incomes fall by 35 percent per annum, principally because of declining availability and quality of land (Marysee et al. 1994, 56–57, 86). In addition, drought (in 1984), excessive rain (in 1987), and plant disease (in 1988) all weighed in to contribute to declining production and food security levels (Ulvin 1998, 57).

As if this were not enough, from October 1990 onward, the country was caught up in a war that was costing an estimated $100 million per annum and was causing massive displacement and disruption, especially affecting the most fertile northern regions of Byumba, Ruhengeri, and Gisenyi (Walter 1993, 12). According to one estimate, the onset of war resulted in the displacement of 15 percent of the population—one million people—and prompted the army to swell in number from 4,000 to 40,000 men (Marysee et al. 1994, 83). Between 1989 and 1991, military spending as a proportion of GDP rose from 2 percent to 6.9 percent (Dorsey 1994, 154).

For all the aforementioned reasons, it is estimated that average GDP per person in Rwanda declined from $355 in 1983 to $260 in 1990 (Uvin 1997, 106), and declined even further, thereafter, as the war persisted. Worsening inequality was by no means solely responsible for the increasingly dire conditions faced by the majority of Rwandans. Mahmood Mamdani further describes the precarious condition Rwanda found herself in the late 1980s and early 1990s when he observes thus "the context of that development was both internal and external. The external dimension feeding the post-1985 resource crunch in Rwanda accelerated with the multiplication of forces that fed it: coffee prices plummeted from 1989; a Structural Adjustment Programme was imposed from outside in 1990, and military spending rose dramatically following the Rwandese Patriotic Front (RPF) invasion, also in 1990. Coffee prices dropped by about 50% in the summer of 1989" (Mamdani 2001, 147).[13]

This went on unhindered in the eyes of the international community. Little or no attention was paid to what was happening in Rwanda. So, from a divisive colonial legacy and subsequent chronic bad governance, Rwanda was plunged in 1994 into a genocide that goes down in the annals of human history as one of the most brutal and unprecedented.

Consequences of the 1994 War and Genocide

The war that began in 1990 and ended in 1994 destroyed the vital macroeconomic and institutional infrastructure necessary for the successful and balanced growth of a modern, market-based economy. Banks were shut down, a significant amount of the money supply was taken out of circulation to refugee camps and the administrative capacity of the government was obliterated. In July, the fleeing interim government took 24 billion Rwanda francs and allegedly substantial amounts of hard currency that had been in coffers of the Central Bank.[14] The amount of local currency looted represented twice that in circulation at the time. The GDP is estimated to have declined by more than half from 1993's already low level as the rate of inflation reached 40 percent.

The new government of National Unity formed on July 19, 1994, found itself with very limited capacity: less than one-third of the civil service and only 3 percent of the professional staff had returned by the end of the year.[15] Reestablishing conditions favoring growth and the development of Rwanda's economy required large investments in training, rebuilding the institutions of governance, and repairing infrastructure. Recreating the public sector provided a unique opportunity for Rwanda's new leaders and development partners to seriously address the inconsistencies and inefficiencies, such as high public wage bills and extensive public involvement in the private sector that had begun to hinder Rwanda's development under the previous regime. The years between 2000 and 2001 mark a significant milestone in the history of post genocide Rwanda. Rwanda had been "classified as a conflict status country from the early '90s until 1998 when the country made significant transition from emergency to sustainable development."[16]

Rwanda's Public Sector Transformation

Rwanda has embarked on an ambitious public sector reform program known as "Rwanda Public Sector transformation and reconfiguration," which falls under the country's current socioeconomic, political, and administrative reforms. This is expected to be realized in the context of the country's dynamics of good governance, whose aim is to deliver quality public service for sustainable economic growth and poverty reduction. "The conviction of the government of Rwanda is that without an effective and well organised public sector, promising priority services and playing a catalytic role in promoting the activities of the private sector, civil society and of other development partners, no development can be achieved countrywide" (Ministry of Public Service and Labor 2004).

Figure 3.3 Kigali Institute of Science and Technology's (KIST) ultramodern laboratory constructed in 2003.

The government of Rwanda has adopted a comprehensive policy framework to guide its own strategic decisions and those of the donors as they worked toward Rwanda's development, especially poverty reduction. The centerpiece of this framework is the PRSP,[17] an ambitious plan to reduce by a half the proportion of Rwandans living in poverty by 2015. The plan's defined priorities and targets are summarized in Vision 2020. The PRSP has been developed in consultation with the people of Rwanda and enjoys broad popular support of both the civil society and the development partners who have aligned their work in Rwanda with the plan's six priorities that are geared toward the promotion of economic growth of particular benefit to poor women and men:

- Rural development and agricultural transformation
- Economic infrastructure
- Human development
- Governance and decentralization
- Private sector development
- Institutional capacity building[18]

Rwanda's Vision 2020 aims at rapidly transforming a depressed agricultural economy into one driven by ICT. The percentage of Rwanda's workforce involved in farming is expected to drop from 90 percent to 50 percent over the next fifteen years. As Professor Calestous Juma has observed, "Rwanda is to some extent doing with technology what Britain did with mechanisation during the industrial revolution" (Rice 2006).[19]

The government of Rwanda envisages the new public sector to have the following attributes:

- A public service that is stable, impartial in its operations, transparent and accountable, competent, and thriving on merit and with integrity, following the ethical values of the Rwandan society and of modern public management
- A highly effective, efficient, and responsive instrument in its size, structure, systems, procedures, practices, knowledge, skills, and attitudes on which the State of Rwanda can rely to execute the will of its people
- A public sector responsive to the needs and problems of the Rwandan population in rendering prompt, quantitative, and qualitative services and supporting the private sector in service provision as well as wealth creation
- A public sector with focused missions, functional light and flexible structures that are in harmony with the missions of the State and that

support efficient, effective, and rapid operations in decision making and service delivery

- A sector that takes the support and facilitation of wealth creation and poverty reduction as the prime goal to be pursued
- A public sector that is results-oriented and capable of fighting the complexes of mediocrity or superiority

The aforementioned attributes of the public sector transformation and reconfiguration are also geared toward the support of the private sector, civil society, and other development actors to create wealth and reduce poverty by providing an enabling environment through effective, efficient, responsive, inclusive, and integrated policy formulation, implementation, monitoring, and evaluation.

To realize the aforementioned vision and mission, the public sector will pursue the following objectives:

In conformity to the new constitution of the Republic of Rwanda, to redefine the roles and missions of the State and its institutions in relation to the roles and missions of the private sector and civil society and create effective partnerships and synergy with them as development partners.

Following the redefinition of the roles and missions of the state and its institutions, it was imperative to review and revise the structures and relationships of the state institutions and agencies, both local and central, in order to accomplish the following:

1. Better align them by establishing effective mechanisms of collaboration
2. Maximize their effectiveness and efficiency, in the production and delivery of services promoting teamwork and synergy
3. Achieve better and enhanced devolution of service delivery functions and capacities to decentralized entities as well as promote delegation within public sector institutions

In light of the now constitutionalized decentralization, to review the size of the public sector, especially central government ministries and agencies, with a view to further decentralize service delivery functions, reduce the size of central government and improve its productivity in terms of the quality of services provided and the role of the private sector as the engine of economic growth supported by an enabling public sector. The right size of the public sector will be coupled with the introduction of new methods of work that will make it more productive and efficient.

In order to improve and strengthen the capacity and performance of the human resource in the public sector, attention will be paid to the following:

- The attraction, recruitment, motivation, and retention of the best talent into the public service
- Right-sizing the personnel in the public service to ensure that the central government and the local governments have appropriate share of human capacities in relation to the decentralized functions
- Reconverting excess human capacity from the public sector to the private sector, which equally needs this capacity given the role it is expected to play in poverty reduction and wealth creation
- Reviewing the structure and profiles of jobs in the public sector with a view to working out a strategy of addressing the imbalances in gender in the public sector as well as providing for the disabled
- Studying the traditional and cultural norms and values of the Rwandan society with a view to selecting the ones that can be integrated into the management culture of the public sector aiming at improving its performance
- To put in place a remuneration structure and system in the public sector that will give incentive for the public servants to be highly productive and support the attraction, recruitment, motivation, and retention of the best brains and skills in the public services while at the same time remaining within the affordability of the national economy

Decentralization Program

Decentralization has been viewed as involving "delegation of power to lower levels in territorial hierarchy, whether the hierarchy is one of governments within a state or offices within a large-scale organization" (Smith 1985, 1). According to the Ministry of Local Government, Community Development, and Social Affairs (MINALOC), "the GOR recognizes that the country's institutions of governance exert primordial influence over society's stability and prosperity and the wellbeing of its citizens."[20] Besides, the policy on decentralization "was conceived in the aftermath of the 1994 genocide when the highly centralized state structures were used to plan and implement the massacres. This highly centralized form of government was a result of both the colonial and postcolonial independence administration, which effectively excluded the Rwandan people from participating in the determination of their own political, economic, and social well-being."[21] As it has been observed, the decentralization process after 1994 was an attempt to "reconstruct the organizational structure of the post-colonial state," which was also part of the Rwanda Patriotic Front's prewar eight-point program, whose aim was to bring the state closer to the people (Musambayi 2005, 145).

The decentralization program, therefore, plays a critical role in the GOR's social, political, and economic transformation of the country. Decentralization has involved the "transfer of responsibility for resource management from the central government to local communities and ensures full participation of the people in the decision making process" (Wamunoba 1995, 237).

The aim of the decentralization policy is to undo the harm that has been caused to local systems of governance by overcentralization (Kisubi 1996, in Langseth, eds. 1996). This harm has been viewed as lying "in the quantitative dimension, specifically in the distribution of authority, responsibility and resources available to central versus local government" (Wensch 1990, 4). Decentralization as a form of measure, therefore, aims to invigorate local and democratic processes.

The first phase of decentralization was from 2001 to 2003, when decentralization was being institutionalized. During this phase, the legal and organizational basis was laid. At the central level, the Decentralization Management Unit (DMU) was established in the MINALOC and the Common Development Fund (CDF). A national policy and implementation strategy for decentralization was published.[22]

Decentralization, therefore, aims to achieve the following objectives:

- To enable and reactivate local people to participate in initiating, making, implementing, and monitoring decisions and plans that concern them taking into consideration their local needs, priorities, capacities, and resources by transferring power, authority, and resources from central to local government and lower levels
- To strengthen accountability and transparency in Rwanda by making local leaders directly accountable to the communities they serve and by establishing a clear linkage between the taxes people pay and the services that are performed by these taxes
- To enhance the sensitivity and responsiveness of public administration to the local environment by placing the planning, financing, and management and control of service provision at the point where services are provided, and by enabling local leadership develop organization structure and capacities that take into consideration the local needs and environment
- To develop sustainable economic planning and managerial capacity at local levels; this will serve toward improvement of planning and implementation of their development programs

- To enhance effectiveness and efficiency in the planning, monitoring, and delivery of services by reducing the burden from central government officials who are distanced from the point where needs are felt and services delivered[23]

Rwanda's decentralization program has been rapid with a number of significant reforms being implemented since the process began in 2000. The reforms have had two goals: deepening decentralization as well as concentration.[24] The second reform in 2005 to 2006 took place within a period of six months and a new structure came in place from 2005 to 2006 with a reduction of provinces from twelve to five, districts from 106 to thirty, and sectors from 1,516 to 416.[25]

One of the main reasons for the second reform is to create more financially sustainable units.[26] Under the new system, a large proportion of the central grant will reach the districts directly, before a large part of grants to districts went through the provinces. This transfer system is designed to equalize partly the financial basis for the local governments (LG) using population, area, poverty, equal share, and performance. Statistical analysis shows that some equalization takes place because of the formula.[27]

In general, the experience with decentralization is new, and different approaches are supported by different donors and organizations.
3.6 Results of the Decentralization ProgramThe decentralization implementation is an ambitious policy geared toward empowering the people of Rwanda at all levels to actively participate in political, economic, and social transformation of the country.[28] The idea behind this policy is to be implemented in a progressive and incremental manner, always taking cognizance of the experiences accumulated and correcting mistakes made.[29]

The first phase of the decentralization program was intended to institutionalize decentralized governance by articulating the policies and legal framework, putting in place the necessary administrative structures, systems, and mechanisms, and holding grassroots and local government elections, among others.[30]

Budgetary Challenges to Decentralization

There have been disagreements between senior government officials over whether or not the central government should determine budgetary allocations to districts or whether the latter should draw their own plans of action. Governors from the newly created regions are not of the view that the central government should first scrutinize the action plans of each district before disbursement of the requested funds (Muliisa 2006).

In a recent revelation, the minister of local government admitted that while there was general appreciation of the improved services at local level to the people of Rwanda, the reforms in decentralization had led to understaffing among ministries and government departments. He indicated that each ministry is supposed to have thirty-five civil servants but currently has less.[31]

Local Government Financial Management Capacities

All districts and towns have developed three to five year district development plans and are now successfully creating MTEFs, although of varying quality. There are still difficulties in submitting them to MINECOFIN, with only seventy-seven out of 106 district MTEFs received for the 2005 budget.

During 2004, substantial training in financial management skills was provided to local government officials; this included training on the manual of procedures, and also on financial reporting. However, low levels of education and literacy continue to slow down capacity building in local governments. District councils in most districts are still too weak to effectively analyze plans and budgets and to provide expenditure oversight. These weaknesses are further compounded by logistical difficulties; for example, normally insufficient copies are made of important local government financial documents.

Moving forward, a new organigram sets out minimum qualifications and salary structures for local government officials. Unfortunately, however, districts and towns are still a long way off from possessing adequate financial and human resources to be able to fulfill this organigram.

Local Government Revenue-Raising Capacities

Most Districts (particularly rural ones) still have a very weak internal revenue collection base, with many unable to afford even to pay staff salaries. Despite this shortcoming, some local governments have been more successful than others in generating their own revenues; in particular, significant success has been enjoyed by those districts that have devolved some fiscal powers to the sector level. For example, in the Ngarama district, the Katabagema sector now collects revenue (especially property tax and fines)—50 percent of which is handed to the district treasury—and manages its own expenditure (it has developed a three-year action plan and MTEF budget). This structural setup has resulted in improved revenue collection and more effective service delivery. The district authorities are now planning to roll out this decentralization arrangement to other sectors. A study of revenue potential in all of Rwanda's 106 districts and towns has been carried out, but unfortunately no comprehensive synthesis of the findings has yet been produced.

Intergovernmental Transfer Systems

More equitable transfer formulas have been introduced both for recurrent CDF budget transfers to local governments; criteria now taken into account include population size, area, presence of income-generating activities (markets, slaughter houses, etc.), environmental conditions, infrastructure development activities, and level of poverty. In addition, CDF capacities are steadily being strengthened, with staff having undertaken training in community-driven development and social accountability, among other things. Moreover, a Royal Netherlands Embassy (RNE)-funded institutional and organizational review of the CDF has enabled a three-year CDF action plan to be drawn up, which aims to increase the efficiency and accountability of the organization, as well as to introduce budget support to districts and towns that meet basic requirements, while simultaneously targeting capacity building to districts and towns not yet meeting these requirements. A number of donors have expressed interest in providing budget support to local governments through the CDF.

However, despite all the previously mentioned achievements, central government grants, which form the main source of local government revenues, remain grossly inadequate and untimely. Indeed, both recurrent and development transfers are still a long way below their mandated levels of 5.3 percent and 10 percent of national domestic revenue respectively, and the frequent lateness of disbursements severely disrupts locally planned activities.

For 2003 and 2004 combined, the CDF received a total allocation of RWF 9.5 billion. However, up to the end of 2004, only RWF 4.6 billion had been committed while RWF 2.7 billion was actually disbursed (Table 3.1). Poor disbursements by CDF reflect a number of problems. First, capacity constraints at district level have led to many project proposals of insufficient quality. To address this, CDF has made a provision of 5 percent that districts can draw from to fund technical assistance to elaborate project proposals. Second, tendering procedure through the National Tender Board (NTB) tended to delay project implementation. To this end, the threshold to involve NTB has been raised from RWF 3 million to 40 million. Third, CDF has been reserving the full amount of commitments against the current year's budget, even though some disbursements would only take place in the next year.

The reduced allocation in the 2005 budget is explained by the funds of previous years, which were not yet committed, to the tune of RWF 4.9 billion. Overall, therefore, RWF 8.4 billion was available for 2005.

Monitoring and Evaluation of Fiscal and Financial Decentralization

Monitoring and evaluation of fiscal and financial decentralization is improving, thanks in part to the establishment of district tendering committees, which procure decentralized goods, services, and works (within set limits and guidelines provided by the NTB), and which present evaluation reports to both the NTB and the relevant provincial administration. In addition, local governments have established function-specific committees at the administrative (cell, sector, district) and facility (health centers, schools, water supply) levels, with diverse stakeholder representation.

This said, there is still a long way to go. The role of provinces vis-à-vis districts (including coordination, supervision, technical support, monitoring and evaluation, and approval of local government activities) is carried out only to a very limited extent, and logistical provisions for monitoring and evaluation remain inadequate. For example, auditors in rural areas often have no access to transport or computers. Furthermore, there is still

Table 3.1 Fiscal decentralization (RWF billion)

RWF billion	2002 (Execution)	2003 (Execution)	2004	2004 (Execution)	2005 (Prelim.)
Total budget of Rwandan ministries	103.20	152.35	134.00	122.13	135.50
Total budget of Rwandan provinces	20.12	25.22	30.50	29.74	33.30
Total budget of Rwandan districts	2.70	5.62	8.78	4.59	11.07
of which... Recurrent Transfer*	1.70	1.53	3.28	2.53	4.07
CDF**	1.00	4.09	5.50	2.06	3.50

* Goods and services for districts = 3 percent of revenue in 2004 and 5.3 percent revenue after 2005.

** Gradually moving toward 10 percent of previous year's revenue. (4.5 percent in 2004 and 5.16 percent in 2005)

Source: Ministry of Finance and Economic Development (MINECOFIN)

no comprehensive and complete fiscal and financial decentralization data set in MINALOC, although the WB has pledged to help set up a simple database in the near term.

Overall Support for Five Year Decentralization Implementation Program (DIP)

In addition to the numerous donor- and NGO-supported projects being undertaken at the district and grassroots levels (and the donor support to the CDF as mentioned previously), many donors are supporting decentralization at the central level, through the provision of institutional support to MINALOC, Rwanda Association of Local Government Authority (RALGA), the provinces, etc. The United States Agency for International Development (USAID) is just coming to the end of a period of support for the local government finance unit in MINALOC, and now the Swedish International Development Agency (SIDA) and DFID are looking to possibly carry on this support, as well as potentially providing funds for fiscal and financial decentralization more generally. Meanwhile, SIDA is also providing support to RALGA, and the United Nations Development Program (UNDP) is funding the national decentralization implementation secretariat, which is the main coordinator and facilitator of the DIP implementation process. In addition, the RNE is supporting the provinces to provide more technical assistance to the districts, and is also carrying out an institutional and organizational analysis of MINALOC. The WB is doing some work on decentralized service delivery; and the SIDA are doing some work on the harmonization of interventions.

CSR Program

The CSR program is under the Ministry of Public Service, Skills Development, and Labor (MIFOTRA).

Through the ministry in charge of public service, the Rwanda government is striving to reform its public service under its general development program and, in particular, within the scope of its strategy to alleviate poverty and in line with the concern for good governance policy indicated in Vision 2020.

However, this reform is undertaken while the country is faced with two major challenges: first, the continuing regional instability due to the presence of Interahamwe guerillas in the Democratic Republic of Congo and second, a highly vulnerable rural population, the highest density in Africa.

Sixty percent of Rwandans currently live below the poverty line, while 40 percent of those live in extreme poverty.

Rwanda's reform agenda was conducted to downsize and reduce state expenditure given the foregoing challenges. On one hand, the government of Rwanda reduced its personnel, proposed voluntary retirement schemes and revised its payroll as well as incentive packages. On the other hand, it introduced the vehicle loan schemes, telephone use reform, and house rent for office use.

In 1998, the first personnel downsizing phase was conducted. A personnel census identified that the civil servants were representing 26.13 percent of salary earners. The rate of 26.13 percent was deemed too huge for a country committed to market-based economy and the promotion of the private sector in the employment creation. From 1998 to 2005, the total number of employees dismissed is estimated at about 8,989 people.

Public service reform is one of the major tools used to transform Rwanda to achieve its Vision 2020. The reform was the initiative to change the Rwandan public administration, which was characterized by highly centralized bureaucracy, duplication and overlapping in the functioning of public institutions, lack of harmonized and standardized administration culture, little focus on results-based management, poor mobilization and utilization of state resources (low absorption capacity and wastage), and high turnover within state institutions due to different pay and management systems. Table 3.2 provides a comparison between Rwanda and other sub-Saharan African countries in the social sectors:

The proportion of households below the poverty line ($1/person/day) was 40 percent in the 1985 household budget expenditure survey and then rose to 53 percent in 1993. It was estimated at 70 percent since 1996 and then rose to 60 percent since 2001.The genocide-related poverty is a particularity of Rwanda. Vulnerability of some groups has increased since the 1994 genocide, resulting in the emergence of the "new very poor" people totally deprived of means and traumatized.

Poor households are now more likely to be female-headed or child-headed and are characterized by a lack of able-bodied labor. The proportion of the households considered "complete" with able-bodied adults has fallen from 86 percent before the war of 1990–1994 to 16 percent after the war, with the remainder made up of female-headed households, widowers, child-headed households, and the elderly, disabled, and marginalized people such as street youth and other disabled.

There has been deterioration in Rwanda's social indicators since the war. It is evident that Rwanda lags far behind the sub-Saharan average. For instance, Rwanda has a per capita income of $240 against $510 for SSA, foreign investment of 0.1 percent against 1.3 percent for SSA, and

Table 3.2 Comparison between Rwanda and sub-Saharan African countries

Social sectors comparison Rwanda SSA average	Rwanda	SSA average
Life expectancy in years	49	51
Infant mortality per 1000 lives births	131	91
GNP per capita in $US	216	510
Foreign direct investment in % of GNP	0.1	1.3
Financial credit to private sector in % of GNP	8.1	65.1
Unemployment % of total labor force	31.1	11.1

Source: MINECOFIN: Statistics Department/Rwanda's Development Indicators, August 2002.

unemployment of 31 percent as compared to 11 percent for Ghana. Comparisons with other countries show that Rwanda has one of the lowest revenue bases in the world.

Given the previously illustrated situation, the GOR's major concerns are twofold: how to raise productivity and revenues of poor households through the creation of jobs and improvement of investments' level for a general growth and how to cope with the regional disparity problem that has resulted as a lack of access to social services. Both of these concerns are in the context of ensuring efficiency and effectiveness in the delivery of services affordable to the population.

The sole reason for which the government embarked on PSR is to enable the sector to effectively support and collaborate with the private sector and civil society so as to create wealth, eradicate poverty, and redress the negative social situation described previously.

All Rwandan state institutions, commissions, parastatals, and public service providing agencies are entirely concerned with public service reform; central and deconcentrated entities (provinces, districts, and towns) are also concerned with the reform.

Achievements of the CSR Program

By early 1999, the government was supposed to establish an independent public service commission to oversee the public service reform, including staffing levels, recruitment, job training, and the organizational structure of ministries. To promote adequate ethical standards, an anticorruption bureau and inspector-general of government was planned to be established during 1999.

Instead of an independent public service commission "the Public Service Reform Program" financed by UNDP was created in 1999.

The Bureau of the Auditor-General for State Finances was created in 1999 to play the role of the inspector-general of the government. In 2003, the Ombudsman Office was created to fight against corruption and injustice.

Table 3.3 shows that 51.6 percent of the workforce surveyed in 1998 is made up of males (19,273) while 48.4 percent (18,275) are females. This is an indicator of gender balance in the Rwanda Civil Service. There are some ministries that have more employees than others. The Ministry of Education (MINEDUC), Ministry of Health (MINISANTE), and the Ministry of Justice (MINIJUST) use about 90 percent of the overall public service staff.

Table 3.4 shows that the number of civil servants holding a university degree (A0) represents 2.7 percent of the overall public service staff. It also

Table 3.3 Distribution of civil servants by employer and sex (census year 1998)

		No. of Employees			Percentage		
ID No.	Employer	Male	Female	Total Number	Total	Male	Female
1	Office of the President	22	18	40	0.1	0.1	0.0
2	Parliament	54	46	100	0.3	0.1	0.1
3	Premature	150	49	199	0.5	0.4	0.1
4	Supreme Court	103	13	116	0.3	0.3	0.0
5	MIFOTRA	83	104	187	0.5	0.2	0.3
6	MIGEFASO	180	178	358	1.0	0.5	0.5
7	MIJESCAFOP	303	156	459	1.2	0.8	0.4
8	MINAFFET	59	33	92	0.2	0.2	0.1
9	MINAGRI	573	170	743	2.0	1.5	0.5
10	MINITRAPE	291	97	388	1.0	0.8	0.3
11	MINAMIT	49	24	73	0.2	0.1	0.1
12	MINECOFIN	148	111	259	0.7	0.4	0.3
13	MINEDUC	13,724	13,936	27,660	74.1	36.7	37.3
14	MINICOM	69	42	111	0.3	0.2	0.1
15	MINIJUST	1,613	637	2,250	6.0	4.3	1.7
16	MININFOR	28	22	50	0.1	0.1	0.1
17	MINISANTE	1,382	2,234	3,616	9.7	3.7	6.0
18	MINITRANSCO	63	40	103	0.3	0.2	0.1
19	MININTER	378	171	549	1.5	1.0	0.5
	TOTAL	19,272	18,081	37,353	100.0	51.6	48.4

Source: MIFOTRA

indicates that the majority (35.5 percent) of the public service staff are holders of a secondary advanced certificate (A2).[32]

Table 3.4 shows also that the number of males (1,985) holding a university qualification (A0 and A1) is higher than the number of females (432) within public service staff.

Considering the aforementioned reality from the census conducted in 1998 general perspectives and reforms undertaken from 1998 to 2005 are as follows.

State Fleet Reform

Before 1999, those holding the post of directors and above had a right to a government vehicle on a twenty-four-hour basis. Ministers had in their possession two cars, one for official use and the other for family.

From 1999, directors and other department heads only remained with the right to one official car during working hours. Transport allowance was allocated from the lowest staff to secretary-general, ministers, and state ministers remained with the official car, but the family car was replaced by a transport allowance of RWF 150,000 per month.

Despite those fleet cost-cutting measures, the state transport cost continued to be high while the country was largely dependent on external financial support with an increasing public debt that has had serious socio-economic consequences for the country.

The GOR has realized that to keep and maintain its fleet—big or small—often amounts to a waste of time, administrative harassment, and irrational use of its budget. Efficiency losses are mainly due to the choice of vehicles, tenders, maintenance, insurance, repairs, theft of tires and spare parts, accidents, major breakdowns, abusive use of its vehicles for personal purposes, and practical consequences on the functioning of the government services when vehicles are immobilized due to breakdowns.

It is in the context of good governance and optimization of state budget allocation that the cabinet meeting of March 2, 2005, decided that the GOR would reduce its fleet to nearly zero, through selling officials' vehicles by auction', and further decided to enable all assignees to access vehicle loan schemes, thereby having their personal means of transportation through the proposed loan scheme that targeted all employees.

Concerning the implementation of the vehicle loan scheme, it is first granted to assignees and later on extended to nonassignees.

Vehicles are bought through loans granted by commercial banks. Each category of employee is eligible to a maximum loan according to the employee's rank.

Table 3.4 Distribution of civil servants by employer, qualification level, and sex (census year 1998)

ID	Employer	A0		A1		A2		A3		A4		No qualification		Unknown		Total
		M	F	M	F	M	F	M	F	M	F	M	F	M	F	
1	Office of the President	6	0	2	2	2	6	1	0	2	2	9	8	0	0	40
2	Parliament	13	3	12	5	11	28	0	4	8	5	10	1	0	0	100
3	Prime Minister Office	23	2	18	0	43	31	13	2	7	5	35	5	11	4	199
4	Supreme Court	7	0	12	1	39	7	17	2	6	1	16	2	6	0	116
5	MIFOTRA	15	3	14	13	30	51	3	21	1	7	18	7	2	2	187
6	MIGEFASO	13	14	25	16	70	109	27	24	3	5	32	7	10	3	358
7	MIJESCAFOP	38	1	20	7	76	52	84	32	14	31	44	15	27	18	459
8	MINAFFET	21	6	8	1	5	12	6	3	3	2	1	0	15	9	92
9	MINAGRI	92	5	35	6	225	83	94	28	4	8	88	26	35	14	743
10	MINITRAPE	39	7	36	2	48	41	14	9	3	8	116	23	35	7	388
11	MINAMIT	13	1	6	1	12	13	2	2	2	5	14	2	0	0	73
12	MINECOFIN	26	2	36	16	34	58	9	16	7	7	18	5	18	7	259
13	MINEDUC	332	41	629	143	5,278	4,588	2,922	2,949	1,066	1,752	2,546	3,400	951	1,063	27,660
14	MINICOM	14	1	7	1	23	19	5	6	3	3	15	12	2	0	111
15	MINIJUST	49	4	68	8	775	292	133	81	62	70	374	127	152	55	2,250
16	MININFOR	7	0	5	2	3	17	1	2	1	0	10	1	1	0	50
17	MINISANTE	99	32	116	75	284	631	119	326	176	609	410	377	178	184	3,616
18	MINITRANSCO	11	2	11	1	13	16	7	6	1	1	10	8	10	6	103
19	MININTER	53	2	54	6	135	106	25	15	8	11	60	20	43	11	549
		871	126	1,114	306	7,106	6,160	3,482	3,528	1,377	2,532	3,826	4,046	1,496	1,383	37,353

Source: Ministry of Public Service, Skills Development, and Labor.

Facilities allowed to assignees to enable purchase and maintain their vehicle are as follows:

- Vehicles are exempted from import taxes and duties.
- The government takes responsibility to deposit on behalf of the beneficiary 50 percent of the amount due to purchase the vehicle.
- The State facilitates the assignee to get a vehicle loan for a balance of 50 percent.
- Vehicles are expected to have a comprehensive insurance cover throughout the whole duration of the loan (five years).
- The State contributes to the operating cost of the vehicle (80 percent) as long as the assignee remains in government service.
- The system of vehicle loan is renewable after five years.
- The government accepted to support 75 percent of the vehicle depreciation.
- In case of moving from the service for personal reasons, the vehicle is withdrawn.

For other civil servants who do not qualify for scheme, state caters for 8 percent rather than 15 percent required by commercial banks so as to encourage and facilitate nonassignees to get their own means of transport.

By the end of 2005, about 2,101 vehicles had been sold through public auction. This exercise generated proceeds valued at RWF 5,106,533,572, or US$9,135,122.66. Only 216 vehicles have remained to serve essential services such as police operations (86), protocol (10), the senior most government[33] and high-ranked officials (5), local government's activities (128), plus utilities such as ambulances not concerned by state fleet reform.

Table 3.5 differentiates expenditures on the assignees and nonassignees fleets. It also shows the expenditure that has been incurred by the state due to the fleet reform. Costs and annual profit are shown. The remaining vehicles are estimated to cause the expenditure to rise to RWF 956,556,873 (US$1,771,193), while the annual profit realized by the state is expected to be RWF 145,143,478 (US$7,415,283.50). This entire amount used for civil servants' fleet maintenance was allocated to more strategic activities for poverty alleviation purposes during the financial year of 2005 to 2006.

Analysis of Table 3.6 shows that the state's expenditures in the first year of the reform, given the balance of the financial statement is negative. From the second year, the percentage profit of the reform increased by 60.86 percent, rising from negative 6.10 percent to 54.76 percent. This is an indicator showing that the GOR will have to first invest considerably where the loss is expected to be RWF 617,729,497 (US$1,105,061.71) for the first year. However, the state will continue increasing its profit by the means of the vehicle loan scheme and by hiring vehicles for its staff missions

Table 3.5 Average of annual costs/annual profit from the civil servants fleet reform (RWF)

N°	Description	State fleet total expenditure (2004)	Assignees reform expenditure	Non-assignees reform expenditure	Expenditure on remnant vehicle	Profit
1	Fuel	6,153,025,221	462,245,533	—	580,824,364	5,109,955,325
2	Maintenance	2,681,176,197	231,122,766	—	253,093,788	2,196,959,643
3	Insurance	269,751,085	218,207,930	—	25,463,572	26,079,582
4	Drivers	1,029,435,372	22,275,000	—	97,175,149	909,985,223
5	Taxes and duties	—	14,189,400	—	—	-14,189,400
6	Location	—	494,361,000	688,431,744	—	-1,182,792,744
7	Loan scheme	—	2,003,390,361	897,463,790	—	-2,900,854,151
	Annual total	10,133,387 876	3,445,791,991	1,585,895,534	956,556,873	4,145,143,478

Source: MINITRAN

Table 3.6 Costs/profits of the state fleet reform over a period of five years

Description	Year 1	Year 2	Year 3 (RWF)	Year 4	Year 5	TOTAL
State fleet expenditure	10,133,387,876	10,640,057,269	11,172,060,133	11,730,663,140	12,317,196,297	55,993,364,714
Reform expenditure	10,751,117,372	4,813,940,910	5,054,637,955	5,307,369,853	4,481,865,499	30,408,931,589
Profit/loss incurred	-617,729,497	5,826,116,360	6,117,422,178	6,423,293,287	7,835,330,797	25,584,433,125
Percentage	-6.10	54.76	54.76	54.76	63.61	45.69

out of the employee's area of employment; the profit gained in the fifth year of the state fleet reform will be equivalent to RWF 7,835,330,797 (US$14,016,691.94).

State Fleet Reform for Private Sector Promotion

The Rwandan state, in the past, used to spend huge amounts of financial resources on its fleet for the different categories of personnel. The government used to spend not only on established civil servants but also on non-established staff, thereby raising the transport expenditure bill.

In general, civil servants go for missions and fieldwork as well as for other duty reasons. Based on projections made for the coming years, the average annual expenditure on missions for employees will cost RWF 1,182,792,744 (US$2,115,908.31).

The GOR has decided to embark on a car-hire scheme in order to meet its transport needs instead of buying vehicles. The GOR has introduced a "zero scheme" with the view to avoiding risks and worries related to the management of its vehicles so as to concentrate on its day-to-day activities.

It is in view of this that the GOR is in the process of securing a partnership with a company that can rent personal vehicles, vans, cars, jeeps, and pickups, for the transport of its employees.

The GOR employs about 1,505 senior staff who need transport either at their place of employment or for missions within the country. For the central government, the market is estimated at about RWF 1,182,792,744 (US$2,115,908.31) turnovers.

Telephone Use Reform

Before the 2005 telephone use reform, the assignees, estimated at 413 officials, had an unlimited ceiling of telephone use either for personal use or office purposes. Some of the high-ranking officials, estimated to seventy-three, had privileges for roaming telephone facilities, which is an expensive system when used to call abroad.

Concerning the telephone use reform, the cabinet meeting held on March 2, 2005 took a decision to cut expenditure on telephone use in government departments and institutions, and they were reviewed and reduced significantly. Table 3.7 shows expenditure on telephone in accordance with staff category.

The State accepted to incur the previously mentioned expenses beforehand while the shortfall would be paid by the consumer. To reduce telephone expenses, it was advised that technology that allows the prepayment

Table 3.7 Monthly Telephone Lump sum (Telephone use reform)

Category of staff	Cell Telephone lump sum in USD VAT inclusive	Fixed line telephone lump sum in USD VAT inclusive
Ministers, State Ministers, Secretary generals in Public Corporations and Commissions	178.89 USD	178.89 USD
Director Generals	125.22 USD	125.22 USD
Heads of Departments	17.89 USD	178.89 USD
Technical Advisors	10.00 USD	89.44 USD
Secretaries at the Ministry of Foreign Affairs and Ministry of Finance and economic planning		178.89 USD

Source: MIFOTRA

system would be adopted. Hence, the consumer would adjust his or her telephone use to the prepayment system. The consumer would adjust his or her telephone use according to the amount of credit available on the telephone.

In this case, the use of the Internet has been given priority. This is expected to increase the efficiency of communication in the public sector and civil service in particular. It will also quicken the information circulation in the whole chain of command. The lump sum provided for telephone calls to officials might not be sufficient to cover their needs in communication. However, it should be understood that the need is ever unlimited while the means remain limited.

Privatization

Privatization is part of a new, broad range of economic reforms that has put the private sector at the forefront of the development process.[34] It has helped reduce government's economic role in many countries and regions.[35] In the case of Rwanda, state-owned enterprises (SOEs) have always played an important role in the economic development of the country right from the colonial era. The WB and other development partners have played an important role in the restructuring of the said SOEs for sale. The financial restructuring includes settlement of liabilities, equity, equity injections, and promotion of financial discipline through elimination of subsidies (Vuylsteke 1988).

Today, Rwanda has sold more than forty firms and the previously dissenting voices have been drowned by the success of some of the privatized firms that are already helping in the development of the country (Vuylsteke 1988).

A study carried out in Rwanda in the 1980s recommended that the country undertake serious restructuring of the SOEs as a precondition for continued aid. Through the WB assistance, the country produced a policy framework for SOEs. The policy framework was reflected in the structural adjustment policy framework that was signed with the WB in 1988.

The broad objectives of privatization include relieving the financial and administrative burden on the government by generating revenue through the transfer and liquidation of government shares to private ownership.[36] Furthermore, privatization has also improved on the efficiency and productivity of enterprises privatized, thereby augmenting the sources of government revenue, reducing the size of the public sector in the economy, and broadening the ownership of Rwandan enterprises.[37]

According to the newly launched investment guide document, the institutional framework for privatization includes the cabinet, which has the final authority over the disposition of public enterprises; the National Privatization Commission headed by the minister of finance, the general management responsibility for privatization; the Technical Privatization Committee, which is responsible for recommending the terms and conditions of individual sales and negotiating bidders; and the Privatization Secretariat, which actually implements the privatization program. The document further states that the government is keen to ensure that the process of privatization is predictable and transparent.[38]

Conclusion

After ten years of privatization, questions are bound to be asked as to how far the exercise has gone. The positive side of privatization exercise is that there has been considerable revenue collection by the end of 2005 to the tune of 36.6 billion Rwanda Francs, translating into a 2.9 percent increase compared to 2004. The increase is a result of expansion in revenue base collections that may be factored by increased investments and private ownership of most former public enterprises.

According to a recent report from the Rwanda Investment, Export, and Promotion Agency (RIEPA), as of December 2005, a total of fifty-two public enterprises had been privatized, generating 7.8 billion Rwanda Francs in cash receipts. However, the report adds that around 87 percent (6.8 billion Rwanda Francs) has been expended, indicating a huge expenditure on the part of the secretariat. The investment guide also points out that most of the enterprises privatized were small, with only four exceeding $1 million in sale price. The largest privatization thus far has been the telecommunications enterprise, Rwandatel, which was bought by Terracom Sarl, a U.S. company, for $20 million. Rwanda Commercial Bank (BCR) was bought at $6.05 million by Actis Group and Banque Continentale Africaine (Rwanda) (BACAR) at US$ 3.37 million by a Consortium FINA Bank Ltd. and Enterprise Holdings Ltd. Most privatized enterprises have been bought by foreign investors. For instance, seven enterprises have been liquidated, with the assets of three of them being sold for about $2 million (RIEPA 2005).

Four other enterprises are in advanced phases of privatization, and another twenty-four are slated for privatization. These last include seven tea factories, two banks, the state-owned Brarirwa, the brewery that is one of the largest businesses in the country. According to the Manasseh Twahirwa, executive secretary of the privatization secretariat, "Overall, privatisation is a success. We have all the time handled sale of entities with diligence and transparency." In the meantime, the Kigali Intercontinental and Kivu Sun Hotels, two government-owned enterprises, have been leased by the Serena Group of Hotels, following a cabinet meeting of October 25, 2006, that "unanimously endorsed Serena Group of Hotels" as the new owners.[39] The two hotels are expected to undergo renovations in the near future.

Rwanda Braces for Bigger Investment Opportunities

As part of its efforts aimed at accelerating rapid national economic growth and development, the GOR through its investment arm—RIEPA—has continued to register remarkable business engagement that, among others, creates for Rwandans several opportunities: job creation, technology transfers, increased revenue, etc.

RIEPA continues to put forth its efforts into attracting more local and foreign investments in the country, and actual results have continued to manifest themselves through tangible investments. The agency also provides business advisory services, project implementation, information and research, export promotion and marketing, investment registration, investment and export incentives management as well as free trade-zone implementation and management.

RIEPA aims at continuously finding more innovative ways of serving our constituency, investors, and exporters better across the range of current and future services, and so, the struggle continues. Amidst all these endeavours, the GOR through RIEPA will improve this year on its investment strategies and, also among other set objectives, host a regional investment conference. Rwanda will also exhibit at an international investment fair.

The First Ever East African Investment Conference

The GOR, through RIEPA, in collaboration with the East African Community Secretariat and the Regional Investment Promotion Agencies/Authorities, organized the first edition of the East African Investment Conference in Kigali, which took place from June 26 to 28, 2008 at the Serena Hotel. The conference was officially inaugurated by His Excellency President Paul Kagame, and more than 800 leading business executives from the East African region including Rwanda, Kenya, Tanzania, Burundi, Uganda, Europe, the United States, and Asia participated.

The conference, whose theme was "*Leveraging the East African Market through Trade and Investment*," was designed to showcase the region's business and investment opportunities and its potential to serve as a commercial platform for servicing the continent since the region has always been perceived as one market. Conference deliberations focused on investment opportunities such as mining, transport and infrastructure development,

Figure 3.4 Rwanda's spectacular flora and fauna. This picture shows an elephant, Mutware, in the famous Akagera National Park situated in northeastern Rwanda, bordering Tanzania.

energy, tourism, ICT, agro-processing, broadcasting and telecommunication, financial services sector, leather goods production, and agro-processing and manufacturing.

The conference, through plenary sessions and one-on-one meetings, provided excellent opportunities for business networking between local, regional, and foreign investors. As a result, new businesses in the different sectors emanated, since investors looked at a bigger market. The forum also provided a platform for the East African countries to deal with the policy issues affecting individual countries, like existing nontariff barriers, etc. RIEPA expects that the forthcoming investment conference leads to increased inflow of foreign and local investments, crafting of joint ventures between the regional block and foreign entrepreneurs, and increased exports and employment opportunities due to increased investments.

The rationale for regional integration is that the formation of economic blocs will foster growth and eventually strengthen economies through the benefits accruing from free movement of goods and services as well as monetary integration. Such free movement of goods and services expands market scope given the concept that borders will "no longer exist" or limit trade. It is this concept that drove the EAC member countries to build East African Community (EAC) as a regional integration bloc.

Regional integration is expected to spur economic development by creating a larger market for goods produced in participating countries, allowing for the operation of comparative advantage in production and eliminating the need to duplicate major infrastructure projects, such as satellite communications systems. It is also thought that by forming supranational institutions staffed by technical specialists, transparency will be increased and corruption diminished. If successfully realized, regional integration would make the various blocs strong enough to be less dependent players in the bargains that need to be made to achieve interregional and, eventually, global integration

Regional economic integration has been almost universally perceived as an essential step to achieving freer world trade. In Africa alone, there are fourteen regional blocs, with half the countries on the continent participating in more than one of them. Despite this dense organizational network, interregional trade in Africa has not moved beyond around 10 percent of total trade. A key reason for this dismal performance is the minimum investments required to produce goods and services even primarily for the region.

Similarly, the EAC, with several investment opportunities, stands to gain from joint efforts to promote investments from within the region as well as from outside the region. The EAC, abound with investment opportunities catalyzed by rich soils and conducive, climatic conditions ideal for a variety of agricultural products like coffee, tea, fruits, and vegetables, is an upcoming business location for many. The EAC has enviable natural assets that make it more attractive than any other region in Africa.

The region is also endowed with a variety of minerals, including fluorspar, titanium and zirconium, gold, oil, cobalt and nickel, diamonds, tantalite, wolfram, coal, and iron ore. This presents an opportunity for development of the mining industry, which is currently underdeveloped.

It is in its continuous efforts to create a strong dialogue between the private and public sector, to create more awareness on investment opportunities, and to create a sound and conducive environment in which the private sector would evolve and strongly contribute to the community's development, that RIEPA plans to organize the first East African Investment Conference.

In the same manner, the conference was organized in a bid to showcase investment opportunities for enhanced dialogue between private entrepreneurs and the top echelons of political leadership in the region and chart a road map for increased investment and export growth as well as a strong coalition for action by both government and industry.

During the recently concluded Commonwealth Heads of State and Government Meeting, member states agreed to jointly organize the regional investment conference to market the region as a consolidated bloc. This will be done through strategic measures to promote East Africa as a business location as well as creating a web portal, "Virtual Trade Fair," for overseas and interregional business opportunities for East African companies.

Japan—African Fair 2008

Rwanda was among the African countries that attended the Fourth Tokyo International Conference on African Development (TICAD IV), which was held in Yokohama from May 28, 2008 to May 30, 2008. The conference was jointly organized by Japan's Ministry of Economy, Trade, and Industry (METI) and the Japan External Trade Organization (JETRO).

The largest event is "African Fair 2008" (May 28 to June 1), where Rwanda was also be among the forty-one African nations that exhibited a range of unique and attractive products under the theme, "Vibrant Africa—a Continent of Business Opportunities," which was proposed by the African Diplomatic Corps in Japan.

It was the third African Fair hosted by JETRO following events held in 1999 and 2006; it will also be the largest in exhibition scale, as well as number of participating countries and exhibitors. African economies have been averaging growth of more than 5 percent in recent years, driven by soaring natural resource prices and increased foreign investment on the continent. Organizers hope this latest event will help further this robust growth by giving African exhibitors a chance to meet face to face with prospective buyers, importers, wholesalers, and retailers in Japan.

The idea is not only to boost African exports to Japan, but also to increase understanding about Africa in Japan. The fair's JETRO Zone will introduce several African products (shea butter, cut flowers, etc.) that are making inroads into the Japan market and have been supported by JETRO programs.

Other special areas and features of the fair include (1) "Japanese Company Zone," introducing the activities of several Japanese firms in Africa; (2) "style AFRICA," displaying African products in a model room setting, showing how they can match Japanese lifestyles; and (3) Organization Booths, introducing efforts by various international and Japanese organizations aimed at supporting African development, including "One Village, One Product" campaigns focused on Africa, under the Japanese government's "New Development Initiative for Trade."

Another major official event that was held in conjunction with TICAD IV was "Africa Symposium," which METI and JETRO are organizing together with the WB, also in Yokohama, on May 29, 2008. Inviting dignitaries from Africa and Japan as well as prominent business figures from around the globe, the symposium will examine Africa's recent growth trends and discuss ways for achieving sustainable growth and shifting economic structures away from overreliance on natural resources. The event also examined ways that private companies can contribute to Africa's development through corporate social responsibility activities.

4

Management of the Public Service Reform Process and the Role of ICT

There is nothing more difficult to execute . . . more dubious of success, nor more dangerous to administer than to introduce a new order of things; for he who introduces it has all those who profit from the old order as his enemies, and has only lukewarm allies in all those who might profit from the new.

—*Machiavelli,* The Prince

The reform of public services in Africa, as it is elsewhere, is based on the idea that a reduced role for the state and increased reliance on market forces will result in improved efficiency and delivery of services

Figure 4.1 President Paul Kagame in an intimate chat with Bill Gates in New York City.

(Ratnam and Tomoda 2005). However, there are many examples of public service reforms whose outcomes indicate the contrary. A key lesson is that reforms can be successful only if they are designed and implemented with the cooperation of, and in consultation with, all the stakeholders who will be affected (Ratnam and Tomoda 2005).

According to the International Labor Organization (ILO), public service reform must be guided by the following basic principles: accountability, transparency, and openness in government policies and actions; the provision of new and better public services; the importance of maintaining and creating good working conditions; and the adherence to core labor standards during the reform process to maintain the morale and improve the performance of public service workers (Ibid.). Furthermore, public service reform is not an end in itself; it is a continuation process to meet changing public needs and conditions. The reform process should work for all, and the success of any reform greatly depends on its objectives, the quality of decision making, and the capacity of all the parties concerned to implement the decisions made. Participatory decision making requires the sharing of all relevant information, the protection of the rights of workers and their organizations, and the investment in human resources to meet emerging challenges. Besides the cut in the civil service, there are indications of improvement in revenue collection, tackling of problems associated with "ghost workers," retrenchment, pay rises, and others. ICTs have contributed in the management of information systems but "problems related to the weaknesses of the state as an impediment to the successful implementation of the reforms remain" (Kiggundu 1997, in Minogu et al., 1997). It is in this context that the challenges to the Rwanda public service reform process are examined.

The public sector reform program in Rwanda has been a result of goodwill from political leadership and development partners who continue to support government efforts in the reconstruction and development of the country. That Rwanda is undergoing a phase of rapid transition is beyond doubt. Looking at the "vicissitudes in the life of a nation, it is tempting to suggest that the single determinant of a nation's growth is the quantum of resources it possesses" (Balogun 2003). The experience of the last forty years or so has demonstrated the one factor that has proved decisive in Africa's development effort is the calibre of available human resource. It is this factor rather than any other that has pushed the continent further on the slippery path of dependence, recession, and economic decay (Balogun 2003).

Rwanda's Vision 2020 emphasizes the importance of human resources in the country's development. In Vision 2020, the country's leadership sets ambitious goals for the nation's development. For instance, Rwanda's per capita GDP is expected to increase from its current level of US$250 to

US$900 between the years 2000 and 2020.[1] To attain this vision will require not only increased production at the national level but also effective implementation of government policy that will require reinforcement of institutional capacity and coordination.[2]

This chapter examines the challenges encountered in the management of the reform process and the important role played by ICTs. ICTs are considered a central pillar of Rwanda's economic growth strategy. This strategy is encapsulated in the country's National Information and Communications Infrastructure (NICI) Policy and Plan (Lwakabamba 2006). Although Rwanda shares a lot with many other African countries, issues related to poverty and weak institutions and the implementation of her ICT policy and plan "presents unique challenges resulting from the social disintegration following the 1994 genocide, which resulted in the destruction of much of the human capacity, infrastructure, and social fabric" (Lwakabamba 2006). Rwanda's case demonstrates "how progress can occur even when the enabling conditions are still weak" (Lwakabamba 2006)."

4.1 Challenges and Constraints

Rwanda's current stage of reforms of her public sector is concentrated on sustaining and deepening the efficiency and improvements, including contracting out noncentral civil service functions to the private sector and carrying out institutional reforms to establish a civil service that operates on the principles of competency, accountability, and transparency and is outward-looking and results-oriented(IMF 2001/2002). It is worth noting that from the time of independence, the practice of public administration has been dominated by western models, "but admittedly when countries have attempted to depart from such models, they have not been too successful either, as state models,"

Over the last twenty years, there has been extensive debate on how to improve the institutions of African states. There is now a welcome emphasis on service delivery and accountability in the use of public money. However, progress has been patchy at best. More than ever, sustained reform depends greatly on the establishment of a domestic consensus on, and an internationalization of, the need for change (Kayizzi-Mugerwa 2003, 54).

4.2 The Role of Donors

The involvement of donors in the public sector reforms in Africa dates back to the 1980s when comprehensive economic reforms designed by the World Bank and the IMF became conditions for 'adjustment loans' and other assistance (Westcott, 1999). The need for political reforms and good governance has been a key element in the bank's discussions with a number of countries including Rwanda.

The most visible donor in the reform exercise to date has been British DFID and the WB. Their support has come in the form of financing the program, which includes making money available for the retrenchment exercise. On the role of the donors, Westcott (1999, 160) advises that "donors should be prepared to assist the CSR management team by providing specialist technical expertise and advice in a facilitative way whilst retaining local ownership. Such support has contributed to the building of local capacity through staff motivation and skills, critical for administrative structures, and participative working methods. Specialized training for change management could also be offered in support of this."

According to a recent evaluation by the DFID, so far the largest bilateral donor to the tune of £168 million, Rwanda has "achieved impressive progress and has put in place crucial policies for propoor growth. Perhaps more than any other country program of recent years, DFID's involvement in Rwanda was driven by a strong political commitment" (Kanyarukiga et al. 2005). According to this report, Britain's strong political commitment to Rwanda underpins the program (Kanyarukiga et al. 2005). Relations between the GOR and the DFID have been very good, though concentrated on a thin layer of top management in government. Contacts and relationships with the civil society and the private sector are much less well developed and present a challenge to the DFID and Rwanda, particularly if the government proceeds with its policy of decentralized service delivery.

The DFID program in Rwanda has displayed a number of clear strengths: a stable political commitment enshrined in a ten-year MOU between the two countries, the commitment to budget support that has helped bring predictability to government finances, flexibility in responses especially during development of the poverty reduction strategy and in the area of public financial management, and the commitment to core government processes. One of the weaknesses of the DFID program, however, is that it is strongly oriented to the support of central government and is not seen to be on the ground.

Aid is still important in reducing the financial and human resource constraint, but donors would otherwise take the backseat (Ibid.). However, because many countries find it difficult to move the process forward, donors will remain important in devising the agenda. It is, therefore, crucial that donors have a clear and effective strategy. The case of Rwanda is particularly challenging given the legacy of genocide and its implications on poverty. Rwanda continues to receive most of her financial support from the United Kingdom's DFID, which is "probably the most innovative of the bilateral donors presently supporting institutional reform in Africa" (Ibid.).

4.3 Challenges of Poverty Reduction

Rwanda still faces a daunting task to achieve sustainable and equitable development. About 60 percent of the country's population lives below the poverty line. While agricultural production has recovered to prewar levels, only 40 percent of prewar industry has resumed production. Rwanda is the most densely populated country in Africa with an estimated annual population growth rate of about 3 percent, now standing at close to 9 million, which, if unchecked, could result in doubling of the population within twenty years.[3] Adult literacy is less than 50 percent. At 205 per 1,000, the mortality rate for children under five is well above sub-Saharan Africa norms and almost half of children suffer from nutritional stunting. HIV/AIDS affects about 11 percent of the adult population. More than 90 percent of the population is dependent on subsistence agriculture on shrinking plots of land of declining quality.

The government believes that the relevancy and legitimacy of public sector institutions at central and local government levels, including the civil service itself, lies in their resolve, capacity, and success in taking the lead and supporting other partners in the private and civil society sectors to work with the people of Rwanda to get out of poverty. The situation of poverty in the country can be summed up as indicated in table 4.1.

4.4 Gender Disparity

Another characteristic of poverty in Rwanda is gender disparity in access to productive assets. In the past, Rwandan women had no legal right to own land. The government recently took a step to correct this disparity by adopting a legislation that promotes gender equality through female access to property rights. In addition, Rwanda today has the highest proportion of women legislators in the world. Women now hold 48.8 percent of the seats in the National Assembly, and the country has come the closest of any country in reaching parity between men and women in national parliament, according to the Geneva-based Inter-Parliamentary Union.

The scope of poverty is also reflected in the relatively poor state of educational indicators. Enrollments for girls are slightly lower than those of boys in primary but are very low at secondary and tertiary education.

As far as poverty is concerned, there are two key issues to be addressed in the Rwandan context: first, how best to increase productivity and

Table 4.1 Selected indicators of economic development and poverty in Rwanda

Indicator	Current level	Year
Population	7.979.930	2000
Proportion of population below the poverty line	60.29%	2000
Life expectancy	49 years	2000
Maternal mortality per 100,000 births	810	2000
Infant mortality per 1000 (before first birthday)	107	2000
Infant mortality per 1000 (before fifth birthday)	198	2000
HIV prevalence (15–49 years)	13.7	2000
Total fertility rate	5.8	2000
Contraceptive prevalence rate	4%	2000
Proportion of children (5 years) completely immunized	72%	2000
Fertilizer used per ha	2 kg/year	2000
Gross primary school enrolment	100	2000–2001
Net Primary enrollment	73.3%	2000–2001
Gross secondary school enrollment	10.2%	2000
Net secondary school enrollment	6.0%	2000
Adult literacy (> 15 years)	52.36%	2000
Adult Literacy (> 15 years females)	47.79%	2000
Adult literacy (> 15 years male)	58.06%	2000
Malnutrition: Low height for age (stunting)	42.7%	2000
Malnutrition: Low weight for age (underweight)	29%	2000

Source: MINECOFIN: National Poverty Reduction Program: The Government of Rwanda Poverty duction Strategy.

incomes of the poor through the creation of employment opportunities and increase of levels of investment for overall growth; second, how best to address the regional disparities of access to social services and provide cost-effective services affordable by the poor.

The major reason for which the government is adopting the public sector transformation and reconfiguration strategy is to enable the sector to effectively support and collaborate with the private sector and civil society to create wealth, eradicate poverty, and redress the negative social situation described above.

4.5 Electoral Democratization and Participatory Politics

A National Electoral Commission was established to spearhead the introduction and support the process of electoral democratization. Elections of district councillors took place in March 2001. The constitutional making process, which was concluded with the adoption of a new national constitution, has determined the nature of democratic practice in the country. The population is already accustomed to participating in determining their development and choosing their local leaders. The success of the elections that have so far been conducted and the high turnout of people to vote indicate potential for successful democratization in Rwanda. There had also been elections at grassroots levels in 1999, which were earlier efforts of people's participation in the electoral process. The promulgation of a new constitution in 2003 and the subsequent parliamentary and presidential elections in the same year indicated that the Rwandan population is politically maturing to practice electoral democracy.

On September 15, 2008, parliamentary lections were held throughout the country. Rwandans voted into office new members of parliament. The election period that lasted three days brought together a six-party RPF coalition against the Social Democratic Party (PSD), Liberal Party(PL) and one independent candidate Jean Marie Vianney Harerimana. The September elections also brought Rwandans living in the Diaspora to participate.

President Paul Kagamewho participated in the parliamentary elections underscored the importance of voting and hoped that this would become a culture. According to president Kagame, the Rwandan elections have "significance in a sense of enhancing and continuing the stability the country has already experienced in the last years"[4]

The parliamentary elections in Rwanda witnessed a landslide victory for the Rwanda Patriotic Front (RPF—Inkotanyi) that took 42 votes of the 53 seats that were contested by all political parties. It will be instructive to note that for the first time in the history of parliamentary elections the world over, women widely outnumbered men. They got 44 of the 80-seat Chamber of Deputies. The percentage of women with parliamentary seats is about 55 percent. According to the Chairman of the National Electoral Commission, Professor Chrislogue Karangwa, the RPF's victory represented 78 percent of the total votes.[5]

4.6 Constitution-Making Process

The government believed that all the efforts it puts into strengthening good governance in the country, which have been hinged on the Arusha Agreements, must be debated by the entire population and the peoples' popular views on how they wish to be governed should be enshrined in a new, national constitution. A Legal and Constitutional Commission was established and spearheaded the important participatory process of making a new constitution. The commission carried out sensitization of the population on the process and guided the population in a referendum that adopted the new constitution, which has now become a landmark in the development of Rwanda after 1994. The whole governance and public sector management are being reconfigured in line with the new constitution.

4.7 Encouraging and Empowering Civil Society

The government, having realized that good governance and poverty reduction necessitate the effective participation of all actors in all sectors, encourages the developmental role and function that the civil society has played in Rwanda. A large number of civil society organizations (CSOs) contribute positively to Rwanda's development, providing services to the population such as health, education and training, and assistance to vulnerable groups. CSOs can contribute to the implementation of government policies and provide constructive criticism to improve the delivery of public services. The media has played a positive role in providing information to the population on issues such as reconciliation and Gacaca, and also helped to promote transparency and accountability within public and private institutions.

4.8 Promotion of Gender Equality and Empowerment of Women

Even if the gender map of Rwanda's governance situation shows severe imbalances, some tangible achievements on which progress can be based have been realized during the twelve years. A Ministry of Gender and Women in Development was created and mandated to spearhead the elimination of gender imbalances in all sectors. The National Women Council, with a structure from the grassroots, was created. The decentralization policy and laws formalized the affirmative action in decision making organized in local governments. A law on succession and matrimonial regimes was enacted improving the rights of women for property ownership. The government ratified the convention on all forms of discrimination against women and is in the process of implementing the Beijing Platform. Gender sensitization campaigns have been ongoing across the country. A National Gender Policy has been designed and a five-year gender action plan adopted. The new, national constitution has made gender empowerment and inclusiveness a constitutional requirement. All public sector institutions beginning with the civil service must be reviewed in their structures, behavior, and human capital to make them conform to the gender-related provisions of the constitution

4.9 Protecting and Managing the Environment

This has been a major concern for the government of Rwanda because it is one of the issues that is core to equity in the country. The government is aware that, as it struggles to extract the present generation of Rwandans from the claws of abject poverty, the well-being and opportunities of future generations should not be compromised. A ministry is in place to champion the policies and programs for protecting and managing the environment. A draft land policy is already written and so is a draft land law. The settlement of some of the Rwandans in "Imidugudu" as a policy is a first step toward reorganizing land settlements to free land for production. It is the duty of the leadership of the country at each and every level, in the public, private, and civil sectors, to lead the people of Rwanda in sustaining an environment that will support their development for generations to come. Public sector institutions as well as the private sector and civil society will have to integrate concerns of environment protection in their policies, programs, and activities.

4.10 Fostering Transparent and Accountable Management of Public Affairs

The government of Rwanda acknowledges that good governance requires public servants at whatever level and in whatever sector to manage public affairs in a transparent, accountable, and responsible manner. The following have been achieved in sustaining the promotion of transparency and accountability.

4.10.1 Office of the Auditor General

To support the'parliament's role of oversight, the government set up the Office of the Auditor General, who generally aims at just and honest reporting on the'government's management of financial and other resources as well as efficiency and productivity in the public service. The institution is also influential in fighting and preventing corruption. However, being a recent creation, it requires a lot of input in terms of building its capacity in order to effectively fulfill its role. In addition it requires to be realigned with the ministry responsible for finance to ensure synergy.

4.10.2 The Media

Another instrument of public transparency and accountability is the press. However, in the case of Rwanda, the press exacerbated tensions among the people through inflammatory print and electronic media. As Russell Smith points out, "the so-called hate media had a significant part to play in the genocide." Today, the government and media organizations have been working together to create a press that can play the positive role of educating and informing the public, thus serving as the public's watch dog. Considering the public debates on issues of national concern held on television, radio, and in newspapers, the press has revamped its image though there is a lot to be done to improve the content and quality of news. A government information policy stressing transparency and accountability is in place. The Rwanda Information Bureau has been rehabilitated. The national radio and television have been equipped. The government has signed agreements with the British Broadcasting Corporation, Deutsch Welle, and Voice of America, among others, to enable them to broadcast on FM radio and TV in the country.

4.10.3 Institutional Building for Effective and Efficient Economic Management

Several institutions have been established to streamline the socioeconomic management in the country. Notable among them are the Rwanda Revenue Authority for strengthening the country's revenue collecting capacity; the National Planning Commission to strengthen the capacity for formulating policies and mobilizing resources; the Rwanda Investment Authority for strengthening mechanisms of attracting local and foreign investment; the Office of the Auditor General of State Finances for ensuring transparency and accountability; the National Tender Board for strengthening mechanisms of government procurement to ensure transparency, economic efficiency, and professionalism; and the Statistics Department to provide credible and reliable statistics for planning. The establishment of these institutions provides a foundation for strengthening aspects of good governance that such institutions champion. The budgetary reforms within the MTEF have contributed to improvement of economic management.

4.10.4 Developing Human Resources and Capacity Building

The government is aware that neither good governance nor poverty reduction will be achieved without the support of a reservoir of Rwandans who are knowledgeable, skilled, and well informed. The efforts toward developing the Rwanda human resources have so far yielded the following modest achievements that could be used as a springboard to develop the country's human resources. The Rwanda Institute of Administration and Management was established and is currently conducting some training for both the public and private sectors. The Institut Supérieur des Finances Publiques is being restructured to offer postgraduate training in finance, banking, and insurance. The Human Resource Development Agency has been created to coordinate policy making in the area of human resource development. There are several universities and institutions of higher learning, some of them initiated by the private sector, that are contributing to the development of the human resource base in the country.

Before the 1994 war and genocide, the Rwandan economy was on the decline. The per capita income had declined from US$380 in 1988 to US$150 in 1994. The social indicators, which were above sub-Saharan averages, deteriorated in the late 1980s.[6] Firstly, to address the challenges of poverty, the GOR in 2002 prepared its first comprehensive PRSP whose aims and objectives were to undertake a full review of the country's first PRSP and related annual progress reports with a view to identifying lessons arising from the impact and processes of the PRSP. Secondly, it was to assess the overall impact and implementation processes of the PRSP. Although Rwanda was ranked one of the top twelve reformers globally by the WB's 2006 Doing Business Report, its overall rank, 139 out of 155, remains low, and further reforms will be needed to reduce the cost of starting a business, estimated at 280 percent of per capita income.[7]

At the social level, access to health services is improving and a new health sector strategy was recently completed to address maternal and child mortality, which, as indicated, above, remain high in comparison with other sub-Saharan African countries. In the education sector, gross primary education has risen rapidly to 131 percent of the school age population, and net primary school enrolment remains at 93 percent, making the target of universal education by 2015 feasible.[8] The GOR has also made the first three years of secondary education as part of free basic education.

A new Water and Sanitation Policy, based on the decentralized approach, was adopted in 2004 and is being implemented as evidenced by the completion of contract models and standards to assist districts in contracting private operators and the promotion of sanitization technologies in rural areas.[9]

Figure 4.2 President Paul Kagame of Rwanda with Bill Gates in New York City during a previous visit by Kagame to the United States.

4.11 The Role of ICTs

The role of ICTs will be dealt with at length in a subsequent chapter, but suffice it to say that ICTs are now seen as "an essential facilitator of service improvement particularly when governments worldwide are facing an increasing trend towards knowledge-based production and the communications revolution."[10] ICTs in Rwanda's socioeconomic transformation is a novel idea whose implementation is government driven. As pointed out recently by Fleeton, the chief executive officer of Development Gateway, "Rwanda is one of the foundation's strongest partners and what distinguishes it is the strong leadership and commitment from the government—from the President himself, from ministers and from Rectors of the hosting institutions."[11]

The introduction of ICTs and their implementation should be examined against a backdrop of post genocide reconstruction and rehabilitation efforts by the GOR. It represents a paradigm shift from the way the affairs of public sector management have been conducted and is in conformity with the reforms taking place that encourages devolution and better service delivery of public services in the context of the country's Vision 2020. The GOR recognized the role that ICTs can play in accelerating socioeconomic development of the country toward an information and knowledge-based economy (Dzidonni 2005, 6). It is on this basis that the GOR made a number of policy commitments[12] aimed at facilitating and accelerating development, deployment, and exploitation of ICTs within the economy and society. The key areas of policy, among others, include the following:

- Policy on creating and facilitating an enabling environment for the development of the national information society and economy
- Policy on implementing special tax packages, instruments, and incentive programs to promote the development of the information economy
- Policy on human resource development and deployment to support the development of the country's information society and economy
- Policy to facilitate the deployment and exploitation of ICTs in the educational system
- Policy on the deployment of ICTs to support the operations of the civil and public services
- Policy on facilitating an investment climate for the mobilization of financial and technological resources
- Policy to encourage and facilitate physical infrastructure development
- Policy on the development of standards, best practices, and guidelines to guide the deployment, exploitation, and development of ICTs
- Policy on creating the necessary enabling regulatory framework for facilitating the deployment and exploitation and the development of ICT products, services, and systems (Ibid.)[13]

Through Rwanda's Vision 2020, the country envisages that the implementation of the ICT 2020 policy framework will progressively reduce the contribution of agricultural sector to the national economy while at the same time increase the contribution of the service and industrial sectors to the economy (ibid).[14]

4.11.1 ICTs and Public Sector Service Delivery

The GOR is committed to the use of ICTs in the efficient delivery of public services as a way of complementing other efforts in the socioeconomic development of the country. The challenges faced by government ministries and departments in the provision of quality services to the people of Rwanda have necessitated the building of an information society. The introduction of e-Government, for instance, has centered on office automation, e-mail, Web access, data communications, and management support (The United Nations Development Program 2004, 13). Already, e-Government applications are beginning to transform the way government is interacting with citizens and the private sector (Mugisha 2006).

4.11.2 The Computerization of the Government Ministries and the Public Sector Organizations (PSOs)

At the beginning of the process, very few government ministries and PSOs have computerized their operations; although, some of them, at the time, have computers in some of their offices, with the majority being used for basic applications such as word processing and in some few cases for spreadsheet and dial-up access to the Internet, which was then limited to just a fraction of the staff. Not many of these organizations were at the time utilizing their computer systems for high-end, value-added applications like information systems Management Information Systems (MIS), Decision Support System (DSS), databases, personnel management systems, accounting, and budgeting systems.

Most of the ministries and the PSOs do not have corporate networks. There was no internetworked system linking the government ministries and the PSOs at the start of the process. The implementation of the programs and the initiatives of the "Facilitating Government Administration and Service Delivery Sub-Plan has changed all this." Below, we review some of the achievements in this area.

4.11.3 Implementation of Organizational Network

On the implementation of organizational and corporate networks, the situation now in the government ministries and PSOs, after close to four years of the implementation of the NICI-2005 Plan, is now very different when compared to what was the case at the start of the process. For example, unlike in 1999 and 2000, the majority of government ministries and PSOs now have in place their corporate networks, with some like the Ministry of Justice having a countrywide area network linking the courts and other judicial agencies.

At the start of the process in 1999, there was no government-wide network interlinking the ministries and the PSOs. A section of a fiber backbone network that could provide the basis for implementing the proposed government-wide network is now in place with the capacity to interlink the Kacyiru cluster of government ministries, the MINIJUST-National Assembly cluster, the PRIMATURE-Ministry of Defense MINADEF cluster, and part of the city center cluster of government ministries and PSOs. Currently, about seventeen government ministries and ten PSOs including one major hospital are now physically connected to the fibre backbone network (Table 4.2).

Table 4.2 Status of connectivity to the fiber backbone communications network

Government ministries currently connected to the fiber backbone network	PSOs currently connected to the fiber backbone network
Office of the President	Rwanda Information Technology Authority (RITA)
Ministry of agriculture (MINAGRI)	King Faycal Hospital
The Senate	National Post Office
Ministry of Justice (MINIJUST)	Rwanda National Tender Board (NTB)
Ministry of Health (MINISANTE)	Rwanda Revenue Authority (RRA)
Ministry of Foreign Affairs (MINAFFET)	The Supreme Court
Ministry of Finance (MINICOFIN)	RIAPA
Chamber of Deputies (National Assembly)	National Security Service
Prime Minister's office (PRIMATURE)	Caisse social du Rwanda
Ministry of Defense (MINADEFF)	RIAM-GITARAMA
Ministry of Infrastructure (MININFRA)	
Ministry of Interior (MININTER)	
Ministry of Public service (MIFOTRA)	
Ministry of Local Government.(MINALOC)	
Ministry of Education (MINEDUC)	
Ministry of Gender (MIGESPOC)	
Ministry of Lands and Environment (MINITERE)	

Source: Government of Rwanda, RITA, *A Review of the Implementation of the Rwanda* ICT4/NICI-2005.

Currently, all government departments and PSOs are connected and are providing a common shared gateway to the Internet for all these agencies.[15] It is expected that this will improve government delivery of services.

4.12 Appraisal of Ministries and Government Departments

One of the major challenges facing Rwanda's public sector institutions is the absence of sound planning units. It is in this regard that in August 2006, a comprehensive assessment of fifteen ministries was carried out aimed at "determining the capacity of ministerial planning units."[16] According to a presidential advisor on policy and planning, the assessment included "analysis on the capacity to plan, compile and disseminate data and information from the ministries' in-house registry or administrative source." Besides, the assessment also provided critical reviews of each institution's progress and hitches in the respective planning departments and would assist in the future planning. As D. Himbara acknowledged during one of the sessions, "most planning units do not undertake evidence based planning processes."[17]

4.13 Conclusion

The management of the public sector reforms in Rwanda has faced considerable challenges and constraints. The reforms are essentially administrative and require continued political goodwill to implement. The reforms have also necessitated the shaking up of, hitherto, moribund administrative setup and introduced institutions that have gone a long way in establishing the culture of transparency and accountability.

5

The Role of ICTs in Rwanda's Development

> All over Africa, there is a significant realization that technology is the wave of the future. African government ministers are travelling around the world—from San Francisco to the UAE to Bangladesh—pitching opportunities for new investors and building deals.
>
> —*Andrew Mack with Jeremy M. Goldberg,* Telecommunications and IT

5.1 Introduction

It is well known that the twenty-first century belongs to the world of ICT. It is a century of knowledge. All over Africa, there is a significant realization that tech is the wave of the future (Katz and Mack 2007). The Internet has even made this knowledge widespread and accessible to anybody who seeks information. Thus, if other technological revolutions such as the industrial revolution had bypassed Africa with impunity, it would be unpardonable for the continent to allow itself to be overtaken by this information revolution.[1] This ICT revolution is the only one that has reduced the entire globe to a miniature world, the global village.

5.2 Rwanda's Approach to ICTs

Rwanda has, in cognisance of this new phenomenon of information revolution, decided not to be left behind and has taken on ICTs with enthusiasm and courage. And this seems to be paying off. A report released by the United Nations Conference on Trade and Development dated October 3rd, 2006, released in New York and Geneva ranked Rwanda top of the league in East Africa. According to Albert Butare, Rwanda's former minister of state in charge of telecommunications and is currently in charge of energy, "this shows that something is going on in Rwanda."[2] In its latest report titled "The Digital Divide Report: ICT Diffusion Index 2005," a United Nations Converence on Trade and Development (UNCTAD) global study on ICT diffusion awarded both Rwanda and Kenya 0.231 points in the global ICT Diffusion Index, placing the two ahead of all the other partners in the East African region. According to Rwanda's minister of state in charge of telecommunications and energy, in about eight years, Rwanda is going to become the ICT focal point in Africa. It is in this respect that Rwanda's policy makers have emphasized the development of her human resources given that the country is not endowed with abundant natural resources.

Rwanda is one of Africa's poorest countries and owing to structural challenges, socioeconomic and political, coupled with conflict and genocide in 1994, had her per capita income slip to US$220 in 2004. Today, about 60 percent live below poverty line.[3] It is against this background that the GOR from the outset identified ICTs as a viable vehicle for propelling the country's socioeconomic development. According to the RITA,[4] ICTs are taking a leading role in Rwanda's development efforts. They have been identified as being integral to Rwanda's growth strategy and as key tools in transforming the predominantly agricultural economy into a service-oriented one.

There is a lot of enthusiasm in Rwanda as to what ICTs can do for the country's development. Many people are overwhelmed with what some experts say about Rwanda becoming the "Silicon Valley of East and Central Africa." It is against this background that the government is determined to transform this country's fortunes by investing in ICTs to realize her Vision 2020.[5]

According to a World Bank report for 2008, Rwanda's commitment to Science, Technology and Innovation (STI) starts at the very top.[6] According to the said report, President Paul Kagame was the first to stress the importance of making science and technology an instrument for the country's economic and social development.

In his January 2007 address to the Eighth African Union Summit, he emphasized that building science and technology capacity is synonymous with economic transformation. STI capacity, he explained, "is about applying science and technology holistically—in all levels of education and training, in commercializing ideas, in developing business and quickening the pace of wealth creation and employment generation, in enabling government to provide better services, and indeed in providing basic tools to society at large for self and collective betterment.

It is not uncommon to find office workers in Kigali talking over Skype, or workers of telecommunications companies like Terracom laying fiber-optic cables that snake hundreds of miles underground and to the top of a 4,500 meter volcano on Karisimbi Mountain, the highest in Rwanda. As if to confirm the faith and determination the government has in using ICTs, cabinet ministers use no papers but laptops during weekly cabinet meetings at the office of the president. This is not an advanced western country but a country that emerged from the horrors of genocide, the fastest in the twentieth century.

5.3 Rwanda's Vision 2020[7] and Role of ICTs

Rwanda is in the midst of an extraordinary development plan to leap into the twenty-first century, in a hurry to catch up with lost years. The Vision 2020 project aims to rapidly transform a depressed agricultural economy into one driven by ICT. If this plan works, the percentage of Rwandan workforce engaged in agricultural activities is set to drop from 90 percent to 50 percent in the next fifteen years. By then the country will be the regional hub, a kind of Singapore of the Great Lakes region. As Andrew Mack and Jeremy Goldberg have remarked, "For all its challenges, Rwanda is by nearly all accounts making tremendous strides, working to rebuild into a modern, knowledge-based economy. In fact a number of Rwanda-watchers these days see the country on track to become the hottest IT spot between Cairo and Durban, a kind of Silicon Valley of East-Central Africa."[8]

In a summit held in Kigali on October 29th, 2007 that attracted nearly 1,000 participants from all over the world, including top ICT companies in the world, President Kagame observed that "in just ten years, what was once an object of luxury and privilege, the mobile phone has become a basic necessity in urban and rural Africa."[9] President Kagame was addressing hundreds of top government and telecommunications industry leaders who attended a two-day, high-level Connect Africa Summit at the Kigali Serena Hotel. At the same Summit, International Telecommunications Union and Microsoft launched Global View, a virtual earth-based online platform to track and help accelerate the implementation of the World Information Society goals in Africa.

While a lot of development of IT and the Internet in Africa has historically been ad hoc, Rwanda decided from the outset to build IT into its strategic plans for the future—in tangible, not just rhetorical ways.[10] After wide-ranging consultations, the government of Rwanda in 2000, launched its Vision 2020, the country's roadmap for socioeconomic development, with a clear focus on IT as a crucial cornerstone.

Part of the choice for IT as a strategy can be seen from Rwanda's position: it is landlocked, with long distances to the sea, troublesome infrastructure in neighboring countries, and chronic instability in the neighboring Democratic Republic of the Congo, and to some extent, Burundi. In a special report titled "Now Mombasa—Malaba Highway Faces Collapse," published in the authoritative newspaper, *The East African*, it was reported that "transport between the port of Mombasa and Uganda could grind to a halt due to the poor state of the main highway connecting the two countries." Although this highway has been in a poor state for a long time, the situation seems to have been aggravated by the persistent rains and the ongoing refurbishment of a section of the road from Timboroa to Nakuru. This state of affairs has affected flow of traffic to Rwanda from the Kenyan port of Mombasa. Besides the costly road transport for Rwanda's imports, it is said that the Nairobi-Kigali air route may be the second most expensive flight per kilometer in the world. This explains why a goods-focused export trade is such a challenging prospect, to say the least. It also explains why building a knowledge-based economy remains a logical and necessary choice for Rwanda.

According to Raphael Mmasi of the RITA, established in 2002 to spearhead ICT growth in Rwanda, the Rwandan socioeconomic ICT development policy and plan development process, supported by the Economic Commission for Africa as part of the Africa Information Society Initiative, began in November 1998. In October 1999, the framework document was released as part of the National Information and Communications Infrastructure, and the policy document was widely referred to as NICI-I (2001 to 2005) and adopted in March 2000 by the cabinet. In March 2005 till June 2005, NICI-I was reviewed and lessons learned became part of the genesis for NICI-II, whose implementation is ongoing (from 2006 until 2010).This is the second stage of a four stage process, part of the twenty-year development program under the umbrella of Vision 2020.

To make Vision 2020 work, the GOR decided to invest in people, especially teachers, and the tools they need. After the 1994 genocide, there was an acute shortage of skilled workers to rebuild the country's technological infrastructure. So, in 1997, the government decided to set up the Kigali Institute of Science and Technology to address the skills gap in technology. Since then, thousands of Rwandan technicians and experts have graduated from this institution, recognized today as a leader in the production of biogas technology as well as renewable energy.

Currently over 1,200 primary schools have computers available. This excludes the secondary and university classrooms that have computers installed. It has been estimated that 10 percent of all Rwanda's secondary schools have wireless Internet access, and plans are already underway to expand this substantially. According to Narcisse Musabayezu, the then Secretary General to the Ministry of Education, by December 2006, the government had given out 4,000 computers to secondary schools around the country. "This combined with a proliferation of private access points—Kigali is home to literally dozens of internet cafes—has put Rwanda on a steep path to integrating IT into every day life and development."

Another boost to Rwanda's ICT program has been the New Partnership for Africa's Development (NEPAD) ICT development strategy, which was first announced in 2003 at the Africa Summit of the World Economic Forum in Durban, South Africa. The NEPAD e-Schools Project focuses on providing end-to-end ICT solutions that will connect schools across Africa to the NEPAD e-Schools network and the Internet.[11]

When President Kagame launched the project in October 2006 at GS Muhura School, Gatsibo district in the Eastern Province, many Rwandans did not have as much optimism as they have today about the fruits they would reap from the NEPAD initiative in the near future.

Given the ever-changing global market demands that need a response from a population conversant with ICT, the project goes a long way to providing a new partnership for Africa's development.

While Dr. Henry Chasia, the executive deputy chairperson of the NEPAD e-Africa Commission, described it as the first time that African governments and the private sector have shown cooperation for an ICT project developed and driven by Africans, President Kagame expressed hope that the strides Rwanda has so far made in the ICT field would supplement the project's objectives. "There is definitely no doubt about our support for NEPAD e-Schools project. Rwanda will build on what has been achieved to date to make the project successful,"[12] he said.

Due to the need to impart modern ICT skills and knowledge to the Rwandan youths, in accommodating the ever-changing information society and meeting the global economic challenges, the NEPAD e-Schools project aims at enabling young people in Rwanda, teachers, and wider communities to tap into the global mainstream of information.

As a result of this effort, the technology will enable the recipients to expand their creativity and hence collaborate with peers across Africa and abroad. The Rwandan beneficiaries will also participate in defining the future of the world they live in, and this will consequently assist in the attainment of the eight United Nations millennium development goals.

The project, a joint venture of the Rwandan Government, Cisco Systems, and Microsoft, is the brainchild of the NEPAD e-Africa Commission. The private companies are sponsoring the demonstration project for a period of twelve months in each of sixteen participating African countries. The partnership with private sector companies, created by the commission for the purpose of fulfilling the objectives of the NEPAD ICT Program, is known as Information Society Partnership for Africa's Development.

Apart from Rwanda, countries participating in this demonstration project include Uganda, Algeria, Burkina Faso, Cameroon, Egypt, Gabon, Ghana, Kenya, Lesotho, Mali, Mauritius, Mozambique, Nigeria, Senegal, and South Africa.

5.4 Challenges Encountered by Some of the Rwandan Schools Benefiting From the NEPAD e-Schools Project

While steps have been taken to achieve the objectives of the NEPAD e-Schools project in Rwanda, some underlying obstacles toward the attainment of the objectives have surfaced.

While commenting on levels of participation between girls and boys in ESSA-Gisenyi, the teachers emphasized that males are more interested in the use of computers per se, while girls are specifically interested in the Internet—both for enhancing their class work and to use e-mail.[13]

In this particular school, a server for the network is there, but has not worked since the school was launched. This is a serious problem as the curriculum content software was installed on the server and therefore is not available to the teachers or learners. They do, however, have Encarta installed on the computers. There is also a copier-printer installed in the lab.

The facility manager, one of the group of teachers selected for initial training, stresses that he needs training in basic maintenance to perform the first level of support—the other two levels being similar to Cisco's arrangement.

Teachers are able to use the lab at any time when it is not in use for teaching a class. However, their use was limited because they have not yet been trained in addition to the fact that the server is not operating.

The teachers asked why there are no laptops for their school, as they are aware that other Cisco schools have some. They seemed unaware of the nature of the demo and the fact that the differences between the consortia models are deliberate.

This demonstrates once again that for ICT to be effectively introduced into schools, the technology must be well maintained, the teachers need ongoing support and training and, most important of all, there must be relevant digital content for teachers to use.

The government has set high goals for spending and investing in IT infrastructure to match the focus on training. For instance, in March 2007, Rwanda committed herself to spend some US$1 billion to build and promote Telecentres aimed at bringing rural areas online and promoting broader-based use of technology for business.

In January 2007, at the African Union Summit in Addis Ababa, Ethiopia, President Kagame reminded his fellow African heads of state and government that Rwanda had set its science and technology spending at 1.6 percent of GDP, bringing it in line with the typical OECD countries, as opposed to other African nations, which average less than 0.5 percent. Thus, Kagame compared the IT future of Rwanda as closer to that of Australia than Kenya.[14]

This optimistic picture of Rwanda's IT industry requires heavy investment and support from the international community, including development partners. A good number of donors have already focused their attention on the IT industry as well as capacity building. Among these is a US$20 million public sector capacity building project, and in 2006, a US$10 million e-Government project, both funded by the World Bank. The goal of these projects is to use technology to overcome logistical challenges—not least in streamlining communications and using video-conferencing to facilitate work with district leaders in different parts of the country. As explained by Albert Butare, the then minister of state in charge of energy and communications, Rwanda wants to use IT solutions to enable local government leaders to function "without them having to come to Kigali all the time."

To adopt ICTs as an enabler of economic development demands a comprehensive approach because of the need to move beyond the requirements of a single sector and facilitate more general deployment of ICTs (Lwakabamba).

6

What Can Be Done?

6.1 What Can Be Done?

Over the last two decades, most sub-Saharan African countries embarked on a series of reforms as a way of improving public sector delivery. While the said reforms are still ongoing in many of these countries, they should be seen as a part of the wider public sector agenda (Peters 1999, 381).[1] While it may be too early to predict their successes or failures, it is clear that they have not been able to achieve their desired results. In a number of African countries, the reforms have not succeeded owing to lack of political will. In the case of Rwanda, there continues to be political

Figure 6.1 President Paul Kagame answering questions in the United States during one of his visits.

will that has resulted into implementation of some of the reforms. Beyond political will and resources, focused leadership is critically important. PSR is an art and not a science (Westcott 1999). The reformers know what they want and how to get there.

The reforms have been based on the WB/IMF recommendations and supported by the same institutions and donors. This factor has tended to undermine the independence of policy makers and has also contributed to the vulnerability of the various countries examined. While Rwanda has borrowed a process from countries such as Mauritius, which has attempted to combine the authority of the state control with the flexibility of the private sector regulator, Rwanda's dependence on foreign aid to the tune of nearly 60 percent of her budget makes her vulnerable. Attempts to reduce Rwanda's dependency ratios are critical to the country's overall development agenda. This partly explains the current search by Rwanda's policy makers for new ways of accelerating the country's socioeconomic development through the use of ICTs to leapfrog the country to development. This Herculean challenge will require not simply hard work but also working smart as well as a paradigm shift in the country's psyche.

It has been argued elsewhere that programs and strategies for Africa's economic recovery and development have not been implemented in full because public sector institutions have been bedevilled by problems of corruption, nepotism, inefficiency, poor coordination, poor management, and institutional capacity and political interference. These weaknesses have stifled the process of socioeconomic development in sub-Saharan Africa.

6.2 Measures to Enhance Ethics and Accountability

Measures to enhance ethics and accountability often feature prominently as part of the agenda of CSR in developing countries. In recent years, the debate on and efforts to curb ethical violations and enforce accountability have intensified in Africa mainly due to four reasons:

- The increase in the incidence of unethical practices and lack of accountability
- The wave of political liberalization that engulfed most of Africa since 1989, which has emboldened a budding civil society into demanding greater enforcement of ethical standards and the punishment of violators
- A growing recognition that unethical practices have contributed to the economic difficulties that many African countries face

- The pressure exerted by international donors requiring stricter adherence by African countries to good governance and the curtailment of waste and squandering of resources

The lack of accountability, unethical behavior and corrupt practices coupled with institutionalized norms of behavior in Africa have become so pervasive that one may conveniently speak of a crisis of ethics in African public services. While one could single out a few countries such as Namibia, Botswana, and Rwanda in which "tolerable" levels of corruption exist, unfortunately the opposite is true in the majority of African countries. Apart from outright bribery and corruption, patronage, nepotism, embezzlement, influence peddling, use of one's position for self-enrichment, bestowing of favors on relatives and friends, moonlighting, partiality, absenteeism, failure to appreciate punctuality, abuse of public property, leaking and/or abuse of government information, and the like are common manifestations of this plight.

The obvious negative impact of such practices on productivity; the responsiveness, legitimacy and transparency of governments; the effective implementation of policies; and the efforts to bring about recovery and development in general dictate that concerted action must be taken by all concerned to deal with this debilitating problem. Dealing successfully with this phenomenon requires a deeper understanding of its underlying causes. It may be appreciated, however, that the matter is not that simple and that political, cultural, and economic factors all lie at the root of this multidimensional problem.

Over time, the state in Africa has evolved as an undemocratic, autocratic, and patrimonial entity being essentially a vehicle to execute the unquestioned will and whims of an unaccountable ruling elite. It became an ideal breeding ground for the very forces making for unethical behavior. Even with the transition to greater political liberalization, overt paternalism is a quality that the state has yet to effectively rid itself of.

Because recruitment in the civil service has been and is still very much influenced by patronage and political factors, the loyalties, commitment, and actions of public officials are often guided and shaped by their primordial loyalties rather than the requirements of impartial professionalism and competence. The sprawling nature of the state, its overextended control over economic matters, and the licensing and approval powers with which public officials are invested have created greater opportunities for the abuse of office for self-aggrandizement.

The issue of whether the economic crisis is the cause or effect of the ethical crisis in Africa is still hotly debated. Nevertheless, one may be of the opinion that while the two crises are no doubt mutually reinforcing, the rapid deterioration of economic conditions experienced by most African countries since the 1980s has further encouraged public office holders, both politicians and administrators, to seek and obtain rewards in exchange for their services. This state of affairs has weakened their moral standing and has affected public confidence and trust in their ability to deliver.

6.3 Is the Situation Beyond Remedy?

Repeated attempts have been made over the years to combat corrupt practices and unethical violations. A common feature of those is the enactment of codes and establishment of institutional mechanisms to enforce ethical behavior.

Nigeria enacted a Code of Conduct in 1975, which was subsequently incorporated into the 1979 and 1989 constitutions, requiring public officials not to allow personal interests to be in conflict with their official responsibilities, not to engage in secondary pecuniary engagements, not to operate foreign bank accounts, not to ask for gifts, and to declare their assets immediately after taking office every four years and at the end of their terms of office. In more recent times, during Olusegun Obasanjo's presidency, there were anticorruption crusades targeting public officials. For instance, in 2005 Obasanjo sacked or charged six top officials with corruption, including two ministers, the senate president, and the inspector general of police. This seemed to echo his 1999 inaugural pledge when he said, "Corruption will be tackled head on at all levels. . . . beneficiaries of corruption will fight back, but we shall be firm with them. There will not be any sacred cows in our crusade against corruption."[2]

In 1957, Ethiopia enacted a Special Penal Code chapter two of which, under the title "Break of Trust and Offences Against the Interest of the Government and Public," covered provisions governing, inter alia, the receipt of ill-gotten gains, misuse or waste of public property, forgery of public documents, corrupt practices, and acceptance of undue advantage. Along those lines, Cote d'Ivoire established an anticorruption law and a "Clearance Certificate Against Corruption" in 1977.

A variety of bodies have also been established to curb ethical violations. Ghana, Uganda, Rwanda, Zambia, Zimbabwe, and a host of other countries in Africa have experimented with ombudsmen. Uganda set up the powerful Office of the Inspector General of Government soon after the National Resistance Movement came to power in 1986. Nigeria established a Public Complaints Committee in 1975 to investigate complaints against public officials, and also a Public Accounts Committee in 1966 to assist the legislature in overseeing the expenditure of public funds.

In Ethiopia, similar bodies were also established in other countries, such as the Working People's Control Committee (1987) and the "Special Court" to try offences related to exploitations, waste, abuse of authority, corrupt practice, and favoritism (1981), and the Anticorruption Squad (1975), the Commission for Enforcement of the Leadership Code (1973), and the Permanent Commission of Enquiry (1966) in Tanzania.

In some cases, these initiatives were partially successful in achieving some of the immediate objectives behind these measures. However, this has not been generally the case. More crucial has been the fact that the incidence of ethical violation has increased even in countries where a large number of violators have been investigated and/or punished. The salient questions remain: why have these measures been generally unsuccessful, and, given the extent of the malaise of unethical conduct and the hitherto limited success in dealing with it, is it realistic to expect that this situation can be remedied?

First, these measures have failed because they were introduced in an overall political and policy environment that was not sufficiently conducive to enable their success. When grand corruption is rampant at the top level of government and politics, the nature of governance has basically remained undemocratic, unaccountable, and patrimonial, and where patronage systems have remained intact, one can hardly expect to enforce measures against unethical behavior with any degree of seriousness unless the enforcement systems and institutions will be left to function without interference. Thus, the nature of the state, governance, and commitment at the highest political level are crucial prerequisites for any successful drive to curb and punish ethical violations. Second, the measures that have been introduced have been partial in nature, focussing mainly on sanctions. Third, many of the institutions that were established to promote ethics and accountability often lacked the resources, public visibility, impartiality, and public support that are critical for their success.

The enormity of the task to deal with corrupt practices and to promote ethics and accountability in the African public service is not to be underestimated. In spite of setbacks experienced in this regard, it is still possible to score gains in a meaningful manner. Central to this possibility is the need for the dedicated and sustained implementation of comprehensive, broad-based and self-reinforcing measures—and not merely partial solutions—by the government and the public to deal with the multidimensional nature of the problem within the framework of democratic, responsive, transparent, and accountable governance.

A comprehensive agenda to promote ethics and accountability in contemporary African public services ought to comprise the following:

- Fostering and promoting enabling conditions of service to enhance professional and ethical standards
- Advancing and affirming sound policies on recruitment, training, and public personnel management
- Encouraging public service associations to play a catalytic role in institutionalizing professional values and defending occupational interests
- Promoting a psychology of service in political and public life
- Creating, strengthening, and upholding the integrity and effectiveness of public institutions of accountability
- Cutting down on excessive centralization and bureaucratization
- Enacting, improving, and effectively enforcing legal instruments, codes of conduct, and regulations as well as promoting ethics and accountability
- Establishing coalitions of business associations and civil society to expose and fight corruption
- Creating mass education campaigns on the extent and cost of corruption and unethical behavior
- Instituting the systematic and impartial prosecution of violators
- Fostering popular participation to ensure the responsiveness, accountability, and transparency of governance

This last element of the comprehensive agenda deserves further mention. Even the best of safeguards and practices under democratic systems of governance can give way to abuses as the experience of developed countries has repeatedly demonstrated. Different observers and theorists often see different reasons that explain why certain countries and not others enjoy a high level of economic development. Many argue that economic development requires some combination of representative government or democracy, a free market economic model, and a general lack of corruption.[3]

For this reason, a crucial safeguard of high standards of public ethics and accountability in Africa has to fall on the ability of the citizens and people's organizations and associations to hold public officials and politicians accountable for their acts and also to ensure that public institutions fulfil their functions properly and responsibly. The ongoing process of political reforms in Africa should enhance such opportunities.

Finally, the international dimension to the ethical crisis ought not to be neglected. Bribery of public officials in developing countries has often been used by businessmen in developed countries as a fair and legitimate method for export promotion. Many governments in industrialized countries ignore the bribery, some openly promote it, and a few even make it tax deductible. There is an urgent need to enforce ethical behavior at the international level if grand corruption in developing countries—including

Africa—as a result of international business transactions is to be curtailed. In recent years, Transparency International has been playing an appreciable role in raising the alarm about this problem and demanding that action be taken to remedy it. Any meaningful progress in this direction would require agreement on and the strict enforcement of international conventions, punishing those engaged in corrupt practices, strengthening international integrity systems, establishing disclosure of external accounts laws, and repatriation of wealth and payments amassed through international corruption. The international community is, however, far from any consensus that is likely to institute such measures.

With regard to institutionalizing good political governance, this would entail an effective separation of powers between the legislative, judiciary, and the executive. There is need, in the case of Rwanda, to put in place at the earliest opportunity an independent public service commission, which was provided for in the 2003 constitution. Most senior appointments in Rwanda are still made by the cabinet, in the absence of a public service commission. In countries where such institutions exist, continued interference by politicians undermines their credibility.

With the support of the public sector or civil service, the executive is mandated to formulate policies, programs, and strategies and monitor their implementation. In most sub-Saharan African countries mentioned in this work, there exists a strong executive that is unable to respond effectively and efficiently to the demands of the people.[4] "It has the constitutional authority and political power to perform its functions, but it does not have the institutional capacities to fulfill those functions efficiently and effectively."[5]

In the case of the civil service, the mandate of the civil servants is to manage the institutions of governance and also advise ministers on a wide range of issues from health, education, transport, and economic growth, to poverty alleviation and others. However, most of the public servants lack the ability to formulate, implement, and monitor policies, programs, and strategies focused on economic growth and sustainable development. One consensus from these reforms is that they have failed to attract and retain the brightest and the best in the civil services (Olowu 2003).[6]

Given the importance of the public sector reforms in the overall development of a country, "mobilisation and harnessing of this resource is very critical."[7] Building critical institutional capacities in Africa for good governance, economic growth, and development is therefore a prerequisite. However, any reform to this end should be carefully formulated, programmed, and implemented, taking cognisance of each country's unique and specific circumstances.

Macroeconomic adjustment reforms that are ongoing in many African countries have not produced the expected results. In recent times, the focus has shifted from retrenchment to capacity building for good governance. One of the most disturbing factors is the relative weakness of sub-Saharan Africa in relation to the rest of the world (Guido and Jemiai 2000).[8] Latin America has, for instance, gone through important changes in her public sector reforms, but in addition to democratization, decentralization, and debureaucratization, the striking element is the increasing participation of the civil society in the public sector. In Asia, the general observation, according to Guido (2000), is the strong tradition of state administration.[9] It would seem to be clear that with respect to Asian countries, they craft their own solutions based on their tradition of respect for authority and deep notion of duty. To redesign and modernize the state institutions to face the new challenges bequeathed by globalization, African governments must first consider and analyze how globalization is affecting the role and functioning of the state.

One of the few ways of bringing about a convergence of donor and recipient interests in Africa is to ensure that donors are partners as they collaborate in providing ideas and funds to jump-start the process in the short run. There will also be need to create a civil service leadership fund to which countries determined to rebuild their civil services can turn for development finance. The condition for the disbursement of such a fund would be improvement in revenue mobilization and progress in those articulated strategic sectors and the installation of the strategic governance structures.[10]

It has been observed that African civil services are not absolutely over bloated but poorly structured. Africa has, according to Olowu (2002), "the least number of civil servants per population among the world's regions." The diagnosis and prognosis of current CSRs, according to Olowu, are equally wrong-headed. The primary task is not to reduce cost but to raise investment in favor of the civil service. There is need to reduce numbers, particularly with respect to the low-paid officials who, in the first instance, should not have been there. There is also need to redefine the scope and mission of the public service organizations such that some of the tasks underpinned by central government organs can be privatized, decentralized, or even outsourced. The emphasis should, therefore, not be on stronger or weaker but on *smart* governments that have strategic institutions that deal with globalization and flexible partnerships between the private and public sectors, as well as national, international, local, and central levels. The recent trends in public sector management are already exerting impact on the character and operations of the public service, and they demand new human resource capacities, professional behaviors, and values. Human resources management and development in the public sector is about people's development and employment opportunities. It is, therefore, critical to provide meaningful careers as well as career paths to individuals choosing to serve in the public interest. What the public sector should bear in mind, especially in sub-Saharan Africa, is that there is competition within a single global market for skills and competencies. The impact of this new shift is likely to be far reaching. New information management technologies are revolutionizing the work of organizations and methods of delivery of public sector services.

All in all, the challenges that confront most of the sub-Saharan countries are derived from a persistent deficit in governance. This poor governance environment underlies the litany of Africa's development problems. The exercise of political power to manage a country's affairs constitutes governance. It is this governance that must be addressed. For the last two decades, Africa's policy makers have grappled with how to resolve the challenges of poverty and move the region forward. The adoption of the NEPAD is one of the ways of fast-tracking the continent's development process. The African Peer Review Mechanism (APRM) constitutes a unique approach at self-monitoring by African countries. Rwanda is among the first sixteen countries to accede to the APRM and the second country in which the review was launched in 2006.[11] For Rwanda it was a historical achievement given the country's harrowing history that devastated the country and its people. Subscribing to the ideals of the APRM further demonstrates that the government and people of Rwanda are committed to improving governance and sharing her experience with the rest of the continent.

Appendix I

Agreement Between the Government of the Republic of Rwanda and the United Nations on the Enforcment of Sentences of the International Criminal Tribunal for Rwanda

Agreement-GOR-UN-Enforcement of Sentences–4 March 2008

The Government of the Republic of Rwanda, hereinafter called the "Government of Rwanda," and

The United Nations, acting through the International Criminal Tribunal for Rwanda, hereinafter called "the Tribunal,"

RECALLING Article 26 of the Statute of the Tribunal adopted by Security Council Resolution 955 (1994) of 8 November 1994, according to which imprisonment of persons sentenced by the Tribunal shall be served in Rwanda or in any of the States on a list of States which have indicated to the Security Council their willingness to accept convicted persons;

NOTING the obligation imposed on the Government of Rwanda by the said Article 26 to enforce sentences imposed by the Tribunal; RECALLING the provisions of the Standard Minimum Rules for the Treatment of Prisoners approved by ECOSOC resolutions 663 C (XXIV) of 31 July 1957 and 2067 (LXII) of 13 May 1977, the Body of Principles for the Protection of all Persons under any Form of Detention or Imprisonment adopted by General Assembly resolution 43/173 of 9 December 1988, and the Basic Principles for the Treatment of Prisoners adopted by General Assembly resolution 45/111 of 14 December 1990;

IN ORDER to give effect to the judgements and sentences of the Tribunal; HAVE AGREED as follows:

3

Agreement-GOR-UN-Enforcement of Sentences-4 March 2008

Article 1
Purpose and Scope of the Agreement

This Agreement shall govern matters relating to or arising out of all requests to the Government of Rwanda to enforce sentences imposed by the Tribunal.

Article 2
Procedure

1. A request to the Government of Rwanda to enforce a sentence shall be made by the Registrar of the Tribunal (hereinafter "the Registrar"), with the approval of the President of the Tribunal.
2. The Registrar shall provide the following documents and items to the Government of Rwanda when making the request;

   (a) a certified copy of the judgement;
   (b) a statement indicating how much of the sentence has already been served including information on any pre-trial detention;
   (c) when appropriate, any medical or psychological reports on the convicted person, any recommendation for his/her further treatment in Rwanda and any other factor relevant to the enforcement of the sentence;
   (d) certified copies of identification papers of the convicted person in the Tribunal's possession.

3. All communications to the Government of Rwanda relating to matters provided for in this Agreement shall be made to the Minister in charge of Penitentiary Administration through the Minister in charge of Foreign Affairs.
4. The Government of Rwanda shall promptly decide upon the request of the Registrar, in accordance with national law and inform the Registrar of its decision whether or not to agree to receive the convicted person(s).

4
Agreement-GOR-UN-Enforcement of Sentences-4 March 2008

Article 3
Enforcement

1. In enforcing the sentence pronounced by the Tribunal, the Competent national authorities of the Government of Rwanda shall be bound by the duration of the sentence so pronounced and in a Prison facility identified and agreed to by the parties.
2. Subject to the provisions of this Agreement and the supervision of the Tribunal, as provided for in, inter alia, Articles 6 to 8 and paragraphs 2 and 3 of Article 9 below, the conditions of Imprisonment shall be governed by the laws of Rwanda.
3. Conditions of imprisonment shall be in conformity with the Standard Minimum Rules for the Treatment of Prisoners, the Body of Principles for the Protection of All persons under Any Form of Detention or Imprisonment and the Basic Principles for the Treatment of Prisoners.

Article 4
Transfer of the convicted person

1. The Registrar shall make the appropriate arrangements for the transfer of the convicted person from the Tribunal to the competent authorities of the Government of Rwanda. Prior to his/her transfer, the convicted person shall be informed by the Registrar of the content of this Agreement.
2. If, after transfer of the convicted person to the Government of Rwanda, the Tribunal, in accordance with its Rules of Procedure and Evidence, orders that the convicted person appear as a witness in a trial before it, the convicted person shall be transferred temporarily to the Tribunal for that purpose, conditional on his/her return to the Government of Rwanda within the period decided by the Tribunal.
3. The Registrar shall transmit the order for the temporary transfer of the convicted person to the national authorities of the Government of Rwanda. The Registrar shall ensure the proper transfer of the

5
Agreement-GOR-UN-Enforcement of Sentences-4 March 2008

convicted person from the Government of Rwanda to the Tribunal and back to the Government of Rwanda for the continued imprisonment after the expiration of the period of temporary transfer decided by the Tribunal. The convicted person shall receive credit for the period he/she may have spent in the custody of the Tribunal.

Article 5
Non bis in idem

The convicted person shall not be tried before a court of the Government of Rwanda for acts constituting serious violations of international humanitarian law under the Statute of the Tribunal, for which he/she has already been tried by the Tribunal.

Article 6
Inspection

1. The competent authorities of the Government of Rwanda shall allow the inspection of the conditions of detention and treatment of the convicted person(s) at any time and on a periodic basis by the International Committee of the Red Cross (ICRC) or such other person or body as the Tribunal may designate for that purpose. The frequency of such visits shall be determined by the ICRC or the designated person or body. The ICRC or the designated person or body shall submit a confidential report based on the findings of these inspections to the Government of Rwanda and to the President of the Tribunal.
2. Representatives of the Government of Rwanda and the President of the Tribunal shall consult each other on the findings of the report referred to in paragraph 1. The President of the Tribunal may thereafter request the Government of Rwanda to inform him/her of any changes made in the conditions of detention as suggested by the ICRC or the designated person or body.

6
Agreement-GOR-UN-Enforcement of Sentences-4 March 2008

Article 7
Information

1. The Government of Rwanda shall immediately notify the Registrar of the following:

    (a) the completion of the sentence by the convicted person, two months prior to such completion;
    (b) if the convicted person has escaped from custody before the sentence has been completed;
    (c) if the convicted person is deceased.

2. Notwithstanding the provisions of the preceding paragraph, the Registrar and the Government of Rwanda shall consult each other on all matters relating to the enforcement of the sentence, upon request of either party.

Article 8
Commutation of sentence, pardon and early release

1. If, pursuant to the applicable national law of the Government of Rwanda, the convicted person is eligible for commutation of sentence, pardon or any form of early release, the Government of Rwanda shall notify the Registrar accordingly.
2. The President of the Tribunal shall determine, in consultation with the Judges of the Tribunal, whether commutation of sentence, pardon or any form of early release is appropriate. The Registrar shall communicate the President's determination to the Government of Rwanda, which shall act accordingly.

Article 9
Termination of enforcement

1. The enforcement shall cease:

    (a) when the sentence has been completed;

(b) upon pardon of the convicted person or upon completion of the sentence as commuted in accordance with Article 8 of this Agreement;
(c) following a decision of the Tribunal, as provided for in paragraph 2 of this Article;
(d) upon the demise of the convicted person.

2. The Tribunal may at any time decide to request the termination of the enforcement of the sentence in Rwanda and transfer the convicted person to another State or to the Tribunal.
3. The competent authorities of the Government of Rwanda shall terminate the enforcement of the sentence as soon as the Government of Rwanda is informed by the Registrar of any decision or measure as a result of which the sentence ceases to be enforceable.

Article 10
Impossibility to enforce sentence

If, at any time after the decision has been taken to enforce a sentence, further enforcement has, for any legal or practical reason, become impossible, the Government of Rwanda shall promptly so inform the Registrar. The Registrar shall make the appropriate arrangements for the transfer of the convicted person. The competent authorities of the Government of Rwanda shall allow at least sixty days following the notification of the Registrar before taking other measures on the matter.

Article 11
Costs

1. Unless the parties agree otherwise:

(a) the Tribunal shall bear the expenses related to:
  (i) The transfer of the convicted person to and from Rwanda;

  (ii) The repatriation or return of the convicted person upon completion of his/her sentence to another country other than Rwanda where he/she is lawfully resident;

(iii) Upgrading of the ICTR quarters in the designated prison facility in Rwanda, upon mutual agreement, to international standards imprisonment conditions under which convicted persons are to serve their sentences pursuant to this Agreement;
(iv) Upkeep and maintenance costs relating to meals, communications, incidentals and special medical care which may entail extraordinary costs in respect of a convicted person who is to serve a sentence in Rwanda pursuant to this Agreement.

(b) The Government of Rwanda shall bear all other expenses incurred in the enforcement of the sentences including:
(i) Safety and security of the identified Quarters for ICTR convicts;
(ii) Prison wardens' remuneration and basic utilities (water, electricity, sewage, etc);
(iii) In case of death, the cost of transportation and return of the body of the deceased to the family members of the deceased, for burial, or if and when necessary, the costs of burial by the Rwandan authorities, in the event that the family of the deceased does not take possession of the body.

(c) Upon completion of his/her sentence, and in the event that the convicted person wishes to be repatriated or return to another country where he is lawfully resident, the Government of Rwanda shall provide the convicted person with all necessary travel documents and authorize his/her exit from Rwanda in accordance with the Rwandan Law applicable to all Rwandan citizens.

9
Agreement-GOR-UN-Enforcement of Sentences-4 March 2008

Article 12
Substitution clause

In the event that the Tribunal is to be wound up, the Registrar shall inform the Security Council and the Government of Rwanda of any sentences whose enforcement remains to be completed pursuant to this Agreement.

Article 13
Entry into force

This Agreement shall enter into force provisionally upon the signature of both parties, and definitively upon the date of notification by the Government of Rwanda of ratification or approval of the Agreement by its competent authorities.

Article 14
Duration of the Agreement

1. Either of the parties may, after consulting the other party, terminate this Agreement by giving at least sixty days' prior notice in writing to the other party of its intention that the Agreement be terminated.
2. This Agreement shall, however, continue to apply for a period not exceeding six months with regard to any convicted person in respect of whom the Government of Rwanda is, at the time of the termination of this Agreement, enforcing a sentence pronounced by the Tribunal.

Article 15
Amendment

This Agreement may be amended by mutual consent of the parties.

10
Agreement-GOR-UN-Enforcement of Sentences-4 March 2008

IN WITNESS WHEREOF, the undersigned, duly authorised thereto, have signed this Agreement. Done at Kigali this Fourth day of the month of March in the Year Two Thousand and Eight, in duplicate, in English and French, both texts being equally authentic.

FOR THE GOVERNMENT OF FOR THE UNITED NATIONS RWANDA

Dr. Charles Murigande Mr. Adama Dieng Minister of Foreign Affairs Registrar of the International and Cooperation Criminal Tribunal for Rwanda [243] United Nations S/RES/1431 (2002)

Security Council Distr.: General 14 August 2002 02-52281 (E) **0252281**

Resolution 1431 (2002) Adopted by the Security Council at its 4601st meeting, 14 August 2002

The Security Council, Reaffirming its resolutions 827 (1993) of 25 May 1993, 955 (1994) of 8 November 1994, 1165 (1998) of 30 April 1998, 1166 (1998) of 13 May 1998, 1329 (2000) of 30 November 2000 and 1411 (2002) of 17 May 2002,

Having considered the letter from the Secretary-General to the President of the Security Council dated 14 September 2001 (S/2001/764) and the annexed letter from the President of the International Tribunal for Rwanda addressed to the Secretary-General dated 9 July 2001,

Having considered also the letter from the Secretary-General to the President of the Security Council dated 4 March 2002 (S/2002/241) and the annexed letter from the President of the International Tribunal for Rwanda addressed to the Secretary-General dated 6 February 2002,

Convinced of the need to establish a pool of ad litem judges in the International Tribunal for Rwanda in order to enable the International Tribunal for Rwanda to expedite the conclusion of its work at the earliest possible date and determined to follow closely the progress of the operation of the International Tribunal for Rwanda,

Acting under Chapter VII of the Charter of the United Nations,

1. *Decides* to establish a pool of ad litem judges in the International Tribunal for Rwanda, and to this end *decides* to amend articles 11, 12 and 13 of the Statute of the International Tribunal for Rwanda and to replace those articles with the provisions set out in annex I to this resolution and *decides also* to amend articles 13 bis and 14 of the Statute of the International Tribunal for the Former Yugoslavia and to replace those articles with the provisions set out in annex II to this resolution;
2. *Requests* the Secretary-General to make practical arrangements for the election as soon as possible of eighteen ad litem judges in accordance with Article 12 ter of the Statute of the International Tribunal for Rwanda and for the timely provision to the International Tribunal for Rwanda of personnel and facilities, in particular, for the ad litem judges and related offices of the Prosecutor, and *further requests* him to keep the Security Council closely informed of progress in this regard;
3. *Urges* all States to cooperate fully with the International Tribunal for Rwanda and its organs in accordance with their obligations under resolution 955 (1994) and the Statute of the International Tribunal for Rwanda;
4. *Decides* to remain actively seized of the matter.

2
S/RES/1431 (2002)

International Tribunal for Rwanda
Annex I

Article 11
Composition of the Chambers

1. The Chambers shall be composed of sixteen permanent independent judges, no two of whom may be nationals of the same State, and a maximum at any one time of four ad litem independent judges appointed in accordance with article 12 ter, paragraph 2, of the present Statute, no two of whom may be nationals of the same State.
2. Three permanent judges and a maximum at any one time of four ad litem judges shall be members of each Trial Chamber. Each Trial Chamber to which ad litem judges are assigned may be divided into sections of three judges each, composed of both permanent and ad litem judges. A section of a Trial Chamber shall have the same powers and responsibilities as a Trial Chamber under the present Statute and shall render judgement in accordance with the same rules.
3. Seven of the permanent judges shall be members of the Appeals Chamber. The Appeals Chamber shall, for each appeal, be composed of five of its members.
4. A person who for the purposes of membership of the Chambers of the International Tribunal for Rwanda could be regarded as a national of more than one State shall be deemed to be a national of the State in which that person ordinarily exercises civil and political rights.

Article 12
Qualifications of judges

The permanent and ad litem judges shall be persons of high moral character, impartiality and integrity who possess the qualifications required in their respective countries for appointment to the highest judicial offices. In the overall composition of the Chambers and sections of the Trial Chambers, due account shall be taken of the experience of the judges in criminal law, international law, including international humanitarian law and human rights law.

Article 12 bis
Election of permanent judges

1. Eleven of the permanent judges of the International Tribunal for Rwanda shall be elected by the General Assembly from a list submitted by the Security Council, in the following manner:

   (a) The Secretary-General shall invite nominations for permanent judges of the International Tribunal for Rwanda from States Members of the United Nations and non-member States maintaining permanent observer missions at United Nations Headquarters;
   (b) Within sixty days of the date of the invitation of the Secretary-General, each State may nominate up to two candidates meeting the qualifications set out in article 12 of the present Statute, no two of whom shall be of the same nationality and neither of whom shall be of the same nationality as any judge who is a member of the Appeals Chamber and who was elected or appointed a permanent judge of the

International Tribunal for the Prosecution of Persons Responsible for Serious Violations of International Humanitarian Law Committed in the Territory of the former Yugoslavia since 1991 (hereinafter referred to as "the International Tribunal for the Former Yugoslavia") in accordance with article 13 bis of the Statute of that Tribunal;

   (c) The Secretary-General shall forward the nominations received to the Security Council. From the nominations received the Security Council shall establish a list of not less than twenty-two and not more than thirty-three candidates, taking due account of the adequate representation on the International Tribunal for Rwanda of the principal legal systems of the world;
   (d) The President of the Security Council shall transmit the list of candidates to the President of the General Assembly. From that list the General Assembly shall elect eleven permanent judges of the International Tribunal for Rwanda. The candidates who receive an absolute majority of the votes of the States Members of the United Nations and of the non-member States maintaining permanent observer missions at United Nations Headquarters, shall be declared elected. Should two candidates of the same nationality

obtain the required majority vote, the one who received the higher number of votes shall be considered elected.

2. In the event of a vacancy in the Chambers amongst the permanent judges elected or appointed in accordance with this article, after consultation with the Presidents of the Security Council and of the General Assembly, the Secretary-General shall appoint a person meeting the qualifications of article 12 of the present Statute, for the remainder of the term of office concerned.
3. The permanent judges elected in accordance with this article shall be elected for a term of four years. The terms and conditions of service shall be those of the permanent judges of the International Tribunal for the Former Yugoslavia. They shall be eligible for re-election.

Article 12 ter
Election and appointment of ad litem judges

1. The ad litem judges of the International Tribunal for Rwanda shall be elected by the General Assembly from a list submitted by the Security Council, in the following manner:

   (a) The Secretary-General shall invite nominations for ad litem judges of the International Tribunal for Rwanda from States Members of the United Nations and non-member States maintaining permanent observer missions at United Nations Headquarters;
   (b) Within sixty days of the date of the invitation of the Secretary-General, each State may nominate up to four candidates meeting the qualifications set out in article 12 of the present Statute, taking into account the importance of a fair representation of female and male candidates;
   (c) The Secretary-General shall forward the nominations received to the Security Council. From the nominations received the Security Council shall establish a list of not less than thirty-six candidates, taking due account of the adequate representation of the principal legal systems of the world and bearing in mind the importance of equitable geographical distribution;

   (d) The President of the Security Council shall transmit the list of candidates to the President of the General Assembly. From that list the General Assembly shall elect the eighteen ad litem judges of the

International Tribunal for Rwanda. The candidates who receive an absolute majority of the votes of the States Members of the United Nations and of the non-member States maintaining permanent observer missions at United Nations Headquarters shall be declared elected;

(e) The ad litem judges shall be elected for a term of four years. They shall not be eligible for re-election.

2. During their term, ad litem judges will be appointed by the Secretary-General, upon request of the President of the International Tribunal for Rwanda, to serve in the Trial Chambers for one or more trials, for a cumulative period of up to, but not including, three years. When requesting the appointment of any particular ad litem judge, the President of the International Tribunal for Rwanda shall bear in mind the criteria set out in article 12 of the present Statute regarding the composition of the Chambers and sections of the Trial Chambers, the considerations set out in paragraphs 1 (b) and (c) above and the number of votes the ad litem judge received in the General Assembly.

Article 12 quater
Status of ad litem judges

1. During the period in which they are appointed to serve in the International Tribunal for Rwanda, ad litem judges shall:

(a) Benefit from the same terms and conditions of service mutatis mutandis as the permanent judges of the International Tribunal for Rwanda;
(b) Enjoy, subject to paragraph 2 below, the same powers as the permanent judges of the International Tribunal for Rwanda;
(c) Enjoy the privileges and immunities, exemptions and facilities of a judge of the International Tribunal for Rwanda.

2. During the period in which they are appointed to serve in the International Tribunal for Rwanda, ad litem judges shall not:

(a) Be eligible for election as, or to vote in the election of, the President of the International Tribunal for Rwanda or the Presiding Judge of a Trial Chamber pursuant to article 13 of the present Statute;
(b) Have power:

(i) To adopt rules of procedure and evidence pursuant to article 14 of the present Statute. They shall, however, be consulted before the adoption of those rules;

(ii) To review an indictment pursuant to Article 18 of the present Statute;

(iii) To consult with the President of the International Tribunal for Rwanda in relation to the assignment of judges pursuant to article 13 of the present Statute or in relation to a pardon or commutation of sentence pursuant to article 27 of the present Statute;

(iv) To adjudicate in pre-trial proceedings.

5
S/RES/1431 (2002)

Article 13
Officers and members of the Chambers

1. The permanent judges of the International Tribunal for Rwanda shall elect a President from amongst their number.
2. The President of the International Tribunal for Rwanda shall be a member of one of its Trial Chambers.
3. After consultation with the permanent judges of the International Tribunal for Rwanda, the President shall assign two of the permanent judges elected or appointed in accordance with Article 12 bis of the present Statute to be members of the Appeals Chamber of the International Tribunal for the Former Yugoslavia and eight to the Trial Chambers of the International Tribunal for Rwanda.
4. The members of the Appeals Chamber of the International Tribunal for the Former Yugoslavia shall also serve as the members of the Appeals Chamber of the International Tribunal for Rwanda.
5. After consultation with the permanent judges of the International Tribunal for Rwanda, the President shall assign such ad litem judges as may from time to time be appointed to serve in the International Tribunal for Rwanda to the Trial Chambers.
6. A judge shall serve only in the Chamber to which he or she was assigned.
7. The permanent judges of each Trial Chamber shall elect a Presiding Judge from amongst their number, who shall oversee the work of that Trial Chamber as a whole.

6
S/RES/1431 (2002)

International Tribunal for the Former Yugoslavia
Annex II

Article 13 bis
Election of permanent judges

1. Fourteen of the permanent judges of the International Tribunal shall be elected by the General Assembly from a list submitted by the Security Council, in the following manner:

   (a) The Secretary-General shall invite nominations for judges of the International Tribunal from States Members of the United Nations and non-member States maintaining permanent observer missions at United Nations Headquarters;
   (b) Within sixty days of the date of the invitation of the Secretary-General, each State may nominate up to two candidates meeting the qualifications set out in article 13 of the Statute, no two of whom shall be of the same nationality and neither of whom shall be of the same nationality as any judge who is a member of the Appeals Chamber and who was elected or appointed a permanent judge of the International Criminal Tribunal for the Prosecution of Persons Responsible for Genocide and Other Serious Violations of International Humanitarian Law Committed in the Territory of Rwanda and Rwandan Citizens Responsible for Genocide and Other Such Violations Committed in the Territory of Neighbouring States, between 1 January 1994 and 31 December 1994 (hereinafter referred to as "The International Tribunal for Rwanda") in accordance with article 12 bis of the Statute of that Tribunal;
   (c) The Secretary-General shall forward the nominations received to the Security Council. From the nominations received the Security Council shall establish a list of not less than twenty-eight and not more than forty-two candidates, taking due account of the adequate representation of the principal legal systems of the world;
   (d) The President of the Security Council shall transmit the list of candidates to the President of the General Assembly. From that list the General Assembly shall elect fourteen permanent judges of the International Tribunal. The candidates who receive an absolute majority of the votes of the States Members of the United Nations

and of the non-member States maintaining permanent observer missions at United Nations Headquarters, shall be declared elected. Should two candidates of the same nationality obtain the required majority vote, the one who received the higher number of votes shall be considered elected.

2. In the event of a vacancy in the Chambers amongst the permanent judges elected or appointed in accordance with this article, after consultation with the Presidents of the Security Council and of the General Assembly, the Secretary-General shall appoint a person meeting the qualifications of article 13 of the Statute, for the remainder of the term of office concerned.
3. The permanent judges elected in accordance with this article shall be elected for a term of four years. The terms and conditions of service shall be those of the judges of the International Court of Justice. They shall be eligible for re-election.

7
S/RES/1431 (2002)

Article 14
Officers and members of the Chambers

1. The permanent judges of the International Tribunal shall elect a President from amongst their number.
2. The President of the International Tribunal shall be a member of the Appeals Chamber and shall preside over its proceedings.
3. After consultation with the permanent judges of the International Tribunal, the President shall assign four of the permanent judges elected or appointed in accordance with Article 13 bis of the Statute to the Appeals Chamber and nine to the Trial Chambers.
4. Two of the permanent judges of the International Tribunal for Rwanda elected or appointed in accordance with article 12 bis of the Statute of that Tribunal shall be assigned by the President of that Tribunal, in consultation with the President of the International Tribunal, to be members of the Appeals Chamber and permanent judges of the International Tribunal.
5. After consultation with the permanent judges of the International Tribunal, the President shall assign such ad litem judges as may from time to time be appointed to serve in the International Tribunal to the Trial Chambers.

6. A judge shall serve only in the Chamber to which he or she was assigned.
7. The permanent judges of each Trial Chamber shall elect a Presiding Judge from amongst their number, who shall oversee the work of the Trial Chamber as a whole.

United Nations S/RES/1503 (2003)
Security Council Distr.: General
28 August 2003
03-48170 (E)
0348170
Resolution 1503 (2003)
Adopted by the Security Council at its 4817th meeting, on 28 August 2003

The Security Council,

Recalling its resolutions 827 (1993) of 25 May 1993, 955 (1994) of 8 November 1994, 978 (1995) of 27 February 1995, 1165 (1998) of 30 April 1998, 1166 (1998) of 13 May 1998, 1329 (2000) of 30 November 2000, 1411 (2002) of 17 May 2002, 1431 (2002) of 14 August 2002, and 1481 (2003) of 19 May 2003,

Noting the letter from the Secretary-General to the President of the Security Council dated 28 July 2003 (S/2003/766),

Commending the important work of the International Criminal Tribunal for the Former Yugoslavia (ICTY) and the International Criminal Tribunal for Rwanda (ICTR) in contributing to lasting peace and security in the former Yugoslavia and Rwanda and the progress made since their inception,

Noting that an essential prerequisite to achieving the objectives of the ICTY and ICTR Completion Strategies is full cooperation by all States, especially in apprehending all remaining at-large persons indicted by the ICTY and the ICTR,

Welcoming steps taken by States in the Balkans and the Great Lakes region of Africa to improve cooperation and apprehend at-large persons indicted by the ICTY and ICTR, but noting with concern that certain States are still not offering full cooperation,

Urging Member States to consider imposing measures against individuals and groups or organizations assisting indictees at large to continue to evade justice, including measures designed to restrict the travel and freeze the assets of such individuals, groups, or organizations,

Recalling and reaffirming in the strongest terms the statement of 23 July 2002 made by the President of the Security Council (S/PRST/2002/21), which endorsed the ICTY's strategy for completing investigations by the end of 2004, all trial activities at first instance by the end of 2008, and all of its work in 2010 (ICTY Completion Strategy) (S/2002/678), by concentrating on the prosecution and trial of the most senior leaders suspected of being most responsible for crimes within the ICTY's jurisdiction and transferring cases involving those who may not bear this

level of responsibility to competent national jurisdictions, as appropriate, as well as the strengthening of the capacity of such jurisdictions, *Urging* the ICTR to formalize a detailed strategy, modelled on the ICTY Completion Strategy, to transfer cases involving intermediate- and lower-rank accused to competent national jurisdictions, as appropriate, including Rwanda, in order to allow the ICTR to achieve its objective of completing investigations by the end of 2004, all trial activities at first instance by the end of 2008, and all of its work in 2010 (ICTR Completion Strategy),

Noting that the above-mentioned Completion Strategies in no way alter the obligation of Rwanda and the countries of the former Yugoslavia to investigate those accused whose cases would not be tried by the ICTR or ICTY and take appropriate action with respect to indictment and prosecution, while bearing in mind the primacy of the ICTY and ICTR over national courts,

Noting that the strengthening of national judicial systems is crucially important to the rule of law in general and to the implementation of the ICTY and ICTR Completion Strategies in particular,

Noting that an essential prerequisite to achieving the objectives of the ICTY Completion Strategy is the expeditious establishment under the auspices of the High Representative and early functioning of a special chamber within the State Court of Bosnia and Herzegovina (the "War Crimes Chamber") and the subsequent referral by the ICTY of cases of lower- or intermediate-rank accused to the Chamber,

Convinced that the ICTY and the ICTR can most efficiently and expeditiously meet their respective responsibilities if each has its own Prosecutor,

Acting under Chapter VII of the Charter of the United Nations,

1. *Calls* on the international community to assist national jurisdictions, as part of the completion strategy, in improving their capacity to prosecute cases transferred from the ICTY and the ICTR and encourages the ICTY and ICTR Presidents, Prosecutors, and Registrars to develop and improve their outreach programmes;

2. *Calls* on all States, especially Serbia and Montenegro, Croatia, and Bosnia and Herzegovina, and on the Republika Srpska within Bosnia and Herzegovina, to intensify cooperation with and render all necessary assistance to the ICTY, particularly to bring Radovan Karadzic and Ratko Mladic, as well as Ante Gotovina and all other indictees to the ICTY and calls on these and all other at-large indictees of the ICTY to surrender to the ICTY;
3. *Calls* on all States, especially Rwanda, Kenya, the Democratic Republic of the Congo, and the Republic of the Congo, to intensify cooperation with and render all necessary assistance to the ICTR, including on investigations of the Rwandan Patriotic Army and efforts to bring Felicien Kabuga and all other such indictees to the ICTR and calls on this and all other at-large indictees of the ICTR to surrender to the ICTR;
4. *Calls* on all States to cooperate with the International Criminal Police Organization (ICPO-Interpol) in apprehending and transferring persons indicted by the ICTY and the ICTR;

3
S/RES/1503 (2003)

5. *Calls* on the donor community to support the work of the High Representative to Bosnia and Herzegovina in creating a special chamber, within the State Court of Bosnia and Herzegovina, to adjudicate allegations of serious violations of international humanitarian law;
6. *Requests* the Presidents of the ICTY and the ICTR and their Prosecutors, in their annual reports to the Council, to explain their plans to implement the ICTY and ICTR Completion Strategies;
7. *Calls* on the ICTY and the ICTR to take all possible measures to complete investigations by the end of 2004, to complete all trial activities at first instance by the end of 2008, and to complete all work in 2010 (the Completion Strategies);
8. *Decides* to amend Article 15 of the Statute of the International Tribunal for Rwanda and to replace that Article with the provision set out in Annex I to this resolution, and requests the Secretary-General to nominate a person to be the Prosecutor of the ICTR;
9. *Welcomes* the intention expressed by the Secretary-General in his letter dated 28 July 2003, to submit to the Security Council the name of Mrs. Carla Del Ponte as nominee for Prosecutor for the ICTY;
10. *Decides* to remain actively seized of the matter.

Annex I

Article 15
The Prosecutor

1. The Prosecutor shall be responsible for the investigation and prosecution of persons responsible for serious violations of international humanitarian law committed in the territory of Rwanda and Rwandan citizens responsible for such violations committed in the territory of neighbouring States, between 1 January 1994 and 31 December 1994.
2. The Prosecutor shall act independently as a separate organ of the International Tribunal for Rwanda. He or she shall not seek or receive instructions from any government or from any other source.
3. The Office of the Prosecutor shall be composed of a Prosecutor and such other qualified staff as may be required.
4. The Prosecutor shall be appointed by the Security Council on nomination by the Secretary-General. He or she shall be of high moral character and possess the highest level of competence and experience in the conduct of investigations and prosecutions of criminal cases. The Prosecutor shall serve for a four-year term and be eligible for reappointment. The terms and conditions of service of the Prosecutor shall be those of an Under-Secretary-General of the United Nations.
5. The staff of the Office of the Prosecutor shall be appointed by the Secretary-General on the recommendation of the Prosecutor.

United Nations S/RES/1534 (2004)

Security Council Distr.: General 26 March 2004 04-28629 (E) **0428629**

Resolution 1534 (2004) Adopted by the Security Council at its 4935th meeting, on 26 March 2004

The Security Council,

Recalling its resolutions 827 (1993) of 25 May 1993, 955 (1994) of 8 November 1994, 978 (1995) of 27 February 1995, 1165 (1998) of 30 April 1998, 1166 (1998) of 13 May 1998, 1329 (2000) of 30 November 2000, 1411 (2002) of 17 May 2002, 1431 (2002) of 14 August 2002, and 1481 (2003) of 19 May 2003,

Recalling and *reaffirming* in the strongest terms the statement of 23 July 2002 made by the President of the Security Council (S/PRST/2002/21) endorsing the ICTY's completion strategy and its resolution 1503 (2003) of 28 August 2003,

Recalling that resolution 1503 (2003) called on the International Criminal Tribunal for the Former Yugoslavia (ICTY) and the International

Criminal Tribunal for Rwanda (ICTR) to take all possible measures to complete investigations by the end of 2004, to complete all trial activities at first instance by the end of 2008, and to complete all work in 2010 (the Completion Strategies), and requested the Presidents and Prosecutors of the ICTY and ICTR, in their annual reports to the Council, to explain their plans to implement the Completion Strategies,

Welcoming the presentations made by the ICTY and ICTR Presidents and Prosecutors to the Security Council on 9 October 2003,

Commending the important work of both Tribunals in contributing to lasting peace and security and national reconciliation and the progress made since their inception, commending them on their efforts so far to give effect to the Completion Strategies and calling on them to ensure effective and efficient use of their budgets, with accountability,

Reiterating its support for the ICTY and ICTR Prosecutors in their continuing efforts to bring at large indictees before the ICTY and the ICTR,

Noting with concern the problems highlighted in the presentations to the Security Council on 9 October 2003 in securing adequate regional cooperation,

Also noting with concern indications in the presentations made on 9 October, that it might not be possible to implement the Completion Strategies set out in resolution 1503 (2003),

2
S/RES/1534 (2004)

Acting under Chapter VII of the Charter of the United Nations,

1. *Reaffirms* the necessity of trial of persons indicted by the ICTY and reiterates its call on all States, especially Serbia and Montenegro, Croatia and Bosnia and Herzegovina, and on the Republika Srpska within Bosnia and Herzegovina, to intensify cooperation with and render all necessary assistance to the ICTY, particularly to bring Radovan Karadzic and Ratko Mladic, as well as Ante Gotovina and all other indictees to the ICTY and calls on all at-large indictees of the ICTY to surrender to the ICTY;
2. *Reaffirms* the necessity of trial of persons indicted by the ICTR and reiterates its call on all States, especially Rwanda, Kenya, the Democratic Republic of the Congo and the Republic of the Congo to intensify cooperation with and render all necessary assistance to the ICTR, including on investigations of the Rwandan Patriotic Army and efforts to bring Felicien Kabuga and all other such indictees to the ICTR and calls on all at-large indictees of the ICTR to surrender to the ICTR;

3. *Emphasizes* the importance of fully implementing the Completion Strategies, as set out in paragraph 7 of resolution 1503 (2003), that calls on the ICTY and ICTR to take all possible measures to complete investigations by the end of 2004, to complete all trial activities at first instance by the end of 2008 and to complete all work in 2010, and urges each Tribunal to plan and act accordingly;
4. *Calls on* the ICTY and ICTR Prosecutors to review the case load of the ICTY and ICTR respectively in particular with a view to determining which cases should be proceeded with and which should be transferred to competent national jurisdictions, as well as the measures which will need to be taken to meet the Completion Strategies referred to in resolution 1503 (2003) and urges them to carry out this review as soon as possible and to include a progress report in the assessments to be provided to the Council under paragraph 6 of this resolution;
5. *Calls on* each Tribunal, in reviewing and confirming any new indictments, to ensure that any such indictments concentrate on the most senior leaders suspected of being most responsible for crimes within the jurisdiction of the relevant Tribunal as set out in resolution 1503 (2003);
6. *Requests* each Tribunal to provide to the Council, by 31 May 2004 and every six months thereafter, assessments by its President and Prosecutor, setting out in detail the progress made towards implementation of the Completion Strategy of the Tribunal, explaining what measures have been taken to implement the Completion Strategy and what measures remain to be taken, including the transfer of cases involving intermediate and lower rank accused to competent national jurisdictions; and expresses the intention of the Council to meet with the President and Prosecutor of each Tribunal to discuss these assessments;
7. *Declares* the Council's determination to review the situation, and in the light of the assessments received under the foregoing paragraph to ensure that the time frames set out in the Completion Strategies and endorsed by resolution 1503 (2003) can be met;
8. *Commends* those States which have concluded agreements for the enforcement of sentences of persons convicted by the ICTY or the ICTR or have otherwise accepted such convicted persons to serve their sentences in their

respective territories; encourages other States in a position to do so to act likewise; and invites the ICTY and the ICTR to continue and intensify their efforts to conclude further agreements for the enforcement of sentences or to obtain the cooperation of other States in this regard;

9. *Recalls* that the strengthening of competent national judicial systems is crucially important to the rule of law in general and to the implementation of the ICTY and ICTR Completion Strategies in particular;
10. *Welcomes* in particular the efforts of the Office of the High Representative, ICTY, and the donor community to create a war crimes chamber in Sarajevo; encourages all parties to continue efforts to establish the chamber expeditiously; and encourages the donor community to provide sufficient financial support to ensure the success of domestic prosecutions in Bosnia and Herzegovina and in the region;
11. *Decides* to remain actively seized of the matter.

United Nations S/RES/1684 (2006)
Security Council
Distr.: General 13 June 2006 06-38491 (E) **0638491**
Resolution 1684 (2006)
Adopted by the Security Council at its 5455th meeting, on 13 June 2006

The Security Council,

Recalling its resolutions 955 (1994) of 8 November 1994, 1165 (1998) of 30 April 1998, 1329 (2000) of 30 November 2000, 1411 (2002) of 17 May 2002, 1431 (2002) of 14 August 2002, 1449 (2002) of 13 December 2002, 1503 (2003) of 28 August 2003 and 1534 (2004) of 26 March 2004,

Recalling that on 31 January 2003 the General Assembly by decision 57/414 A and in accordance with Article 12 bis, paragraph 1 (b) of the Statute of the International Tribunal for Rwanda, as amended, elected from a list of candidates approved by resolution 1449 (2002) of 13 December 2002, the following eleven judges to a four-year term of office at the International Tribunal beginning on 25 May 2003 and to end on 24 May 2007: Mr. Mansoor Ahmed (Pakistan);

Mr. Sergei Aleckseievich Egorov (Russian Federation); Mr. Asoka Zoysa

Gunawardena (Sri Lanka); Mr. Mehmet Güney (Turkey); Mr. Erik Møse (Norway);

Ms. Arlete Ramaroson (Madagascar); Mr. Jai Ram Reddy (Fiji); Mr. William

Hussein Sekule (United Republic of Tanzania); Ms. Andrésa Vaz (Senegal);

Ms. Inés Mónica Weinberg de Roca (Argentina) and Mr. Lloyd George Williams (Saint Kitts and Nevis),

Recalling that when Mr. Mansoor Ahmed resigned, the Secretary-General, after consultations with the Security Council and the General Assembly and in accordance with Article 12 bis, paragraph 2 of the Tribunal's Statute, appointed Ms. Khalida Rachid Khan of Pakistan effective as of 7 July 2003, for the remainder of Judge Ahmed's term of office,

Recalling that when Mr. Lloyd George Williams resigned, the Secretary-General after consultations with the Security Council and the General Assembly and in accordance with Article 12 bis, paragraph 2 of the Tribunal's Statute, appointed Sir Charles Michael Dennis Byron of Saint Kitts and Nevis effective as of 8 April 2004 for the remainder of Mr. Williams' term of office,

Recalling that when Mr. Asoka Zoysa Gunawardena resigned, the Secretary-General, after consultations with the Security Council and the General Assembly and in accordance with Article 12 bis, paragraph 2 of the Tribunal's Statute,

appointed Mr. Asoka de Silva of Sri Lanka effective as of 2 August 2004 for the remainder of Mr. Gunawardena's term of office,

Taking note of the letter to the President of the Security Council from the Secretary-General dated 3 May 2006,

Decides in response to the request by the Secretary-General and notwithstanding the provisions of Article 12 (bis), of the Statute of the International Tribunal for Rwanda, to extend the term of office of the following permanent judges of the International Tribunal at the Tribunal until 31 December 2008:

- Mr. Charles Michael Dennis Byron (Saint Kitts and Nevis)
- Mr. Asoka de Silva (Sri Lanka)
- Mr. Sergei Aleckseievich Egorov (Russian Federation)
- Mr. Mehmet Güney (Turkey)
- Ms. Khalida Rachid Khan (Pakistan)
- Mr. Erik Møse (Norway)
- Ms. Arlete Ramaroson (Madagascar)
- Mr. Jai Ram Reddy (Fiji)
- Mr. William Hussein Sekule (United Republic of Tanzania)
- Ms. Andrésa Vaz (Senegal)
- Ms. Inés Mónica Weinberg de Roca (Argentina)

Requests States, to continue to make every effort to ensure that their nationals who serve as permanent judges of the International Tribunal for Rwanda, remain available to serve in their positions until 31 December 2008.

United Nations S/RES/1717 (2006)

Security Council

Distr.: General 13 October 2006 06-57058 (E)

0657058

Resolution 1717 (2006)

Adopted by the Security Council at its 5550th meeting, on 13 October 2006

The Security Council,

Recalling its resolutions 955 (1994) of 8 November 1994, 1165 (1998) of 30 April 1998, 1329 (2000) of 30 November 2000, 1411 (2002) of 17 May 2002, 1431 (2002) of 14 August 2002, 1449 (2002) of 13 December 2002, 1503 (2003) of 28 August 2003 and 1534 (2004) of 26 March 2004,

Recalling that on 25 June 2003, the General Assembly by its decision 57/414 and in accordance with Article 12 ter, paragraph 1 (d) of the International Tribunal for Rwanda's Statute, elected from a list of candidates approved by the Security Council the following eighteen ad litem judges to a four-year term of office beginning on 25 June 2003 and to end on 24 June 2007: Mr. Aydin Sefa Akay

(Turkey); Ms. Florence Rita Arrey (Cameroon); Ms. Solomy Balungi Bossa

(Uganda); Mr. Robert Fremr (Czech Republic); Ms. Taghrid Hikmet (Jordan);

Ms. Karin Hökborg (Sweden); Mr. Vagn Joensen (Denmark); Mr. Gberdao Gustave

Kam (Burkina Faso); Ms. Flavia Lattanzi (Italy); Mr. Kenneth Machin (United

Kingdom); Mr. Joseph Edward Chiondo Masanche (United Republic of Tanzania);

Mr. Tan Sri Dato' Hj. Mohd. Azmi Dato' Hj. Kamaruddin (Malaysia); Mr. Lee

Gacuiga Muthoga (Kenya); Mr. Seon Ki Park (Republic of Korea); Mr. Mparany

Mamy Richard Rajohnson (Madagascar); Mr. Emile Francis Short (Ghana);

Mr. Albertus Henricus Johannes Swart (Netherlands); and Ms. Aura E. Guerra de Villalaz (Panama),

Recalling that the Security Council by its resolution 1684 (2006) of 13 June 2006 extended the terms of the eleven permanent judges serving at the International Tribunal for Rwanda until 31 December 2008,

Recalling that the Security Council by its resolution 1705 (2006) of 29 August 2006 decided, notwithstanding the provisions of Article 12 ter of the Statute of the International Tribunal for Rwanda, and notwithstanding that Judge Bossa's elected term as an ad litem judge of the International Tribunal will end on 24 June 2007, to authorize her, effective 28 August 2006, to continue to serve as a judge in the *Butare* case until its completion,

Taking note of the letter to the President of the Security Council from the Secretary-General dated 2 October 2006, S/RES/1717 (2006) 06-57058 2

1. *Decides* in response to the request by the Secretary-General and notwithstanding the provisions of Article 12 ter of the Statute of the International Tribunal for Rwanda, to extend until 31 December 2008 the term of office of the following ad litem judges of the International Tribunal who were elected on 25 June 2003:

- Mr. Aydin Sefa Akay (Turkey);
- Ms. Florence Rita Arrey (Cameroon);
- Ms. Solomy Balungi Bossa (Uganda);
- Mr. Robert Fremr (Czech Republic);
- Ms. Taghrid Hikmet (Jordan);
- Ms. Karin Hökborg (Sweden);
- Mr. Vagn Joensen (Denmark);
- Mr. Gberdao Gustave Kam (Burkina Faso);
- Ms. Flavia Lattanzi (Italy);
- Mr. Kenneth Machin (United Kingdom);
- Mr. Joseph Edward Chiondo Masanche (United Republic of Tanzania);
- Mr. Tan Sri Dato' Hj. Mohd. Azmi Dato' Hj. Kamaruddin (Malaysia);
- Mr. Lee Gacuiga Muthoga (Kenya);
- Mr. Seon Ki Park (Republic of Korea);
- Mr. Mparany Mamy Richard Rajohnson (Madagascar);
- Mr. Emile Francis Short (Ghana);
- Mr. Albertus Henricus Johannes Swart (Netherlands);
- Ms. Aura E. Guerra de Villalaz (Panama).

2. *Decides* in response to the request by the Secretary-General to allow ad litem Judges Bossa, Arrey, Lattanzi, Muthoga, Short, Hökborg, Hikmet, Kam and Park to serve in the International Tribunal for Rwanda beyond the cumulative period of service provided for under Article 12 ter of the Statute and until 31 December 2008;

3. *Requests* States to continue to make every effort to ensure that their nationals who were elected as ad litem judges of the International Tribunal for Rwanda remain available to serve until 31 December 2008;
4. *Decides* to remain seized of the matter.

United Nations S/RES/1717 (2006) **Security Council**
Distr.: General 13 October 2006 06-57058 (E) ***0657058***

Resolution 1717 (2006) Adopted by the Security Council at its 5550th meeting, on 13 October 2006

The Security Council,

Recalling its resolutions 955 (1994) of 8 November 1994, 1165 (1998) of 30 April 1998, 1329 (2000) of 30 November 2000, 1411 (2002) of 17 May 2002, 1431 (2002) of 14 August 2002, 1449 (2002) of 13 December 2002, 1503 (2003) of 28 August 2003 and 1534 (2004) of 26 March 2004,

Recalling that on 25 June 2003, the General Assembly by its decision 57/414 and in accordance with Article 12 ter, paragraph 1 (d) of the International Tribunal for Rwanda's Statute, elected from a list of candidates approved by the Security Council the following eighteen ad litem judges to a four-year term of office beginning on 25 June 2003 and to end on 24 June 2007: Mr. Aydin Sefa Akay

(Turkey); Ms. Florence Rita Arrey (Cameroon); Ms. Solomy Balungi Bossa

(Uganda); Mr. Robert Fremr (Czech Republic); Ms. Taghrid Hikmet (Jordan);

Ms. Karin Hökborg (Sweden); Mr. Vagn Joensen (Denmark); Mr. Gberdao Gustave

Kam (Burkina Faso); Ms. Flavia Lattanzi (Italy); Mr. Kenneth Machin (United

Kingdom); Mr. Joseph Edward Chiondo Masanche (United Republic of Tanzania);

Mr. Tan Sri Dato' Hj. Mohd. Azmi Dato' Hj. Kamaruddin (Malaysia); Mr. Lee

Gacuiga Muthoga (Kenya); Mr. Seon Ki Park (Republic of Korea); Mr. Mparany

Mamy Richard Rajohnson (Madagascar); Mr. Emile Francis Short (Ghana);

Mr. Albertus Henricus Johannes Swart (Netherlands); and Ms. Aura E. Guerra de Villalaz (Panama),

Recalling that the Security Council by its resolution 1684 (2006) of 13 June 2006 extended the terms of the eleven permanent judges serving at the International Tribunal for Rwanda until 31 December 2008,

Recalling that the Security Council by its resolution 1705 (2006) of 29 August 2006 decided, notwithstanding the provisions of Article 12 ter of the Statute of the International Tribunal for Rwanda, and notwithstanding that Judge Bossa's elected term as an ad litem judge of the International Tribunal will end on 24 June 2007, to authorize her, effective 28 August 2006, to continue to serve as a judge in the *Butare*

case until its completion,

Taking note of the letter to the President of the Security Council from the

Secretary-General dated 2 October 2006,

S/RES/1717 (2006)

06-57058 **2**

1. *Decides* in response to the request by the Secretary-General and notwithstanding the provisions of Article 12 ter of the Statute of the International Tribunal for Rwanda, to extend until 31 December 2008 the term of office of the following ad litem judges of the International Tribunal who were elected on 25 June 2003:

- Mr. Aydin Sefa Akay (Turkey);
- Ms. Florence Rita Arrey (Cameroon);
- Ms. Solomy Balungi Bossa (Uganda);
- Mr. Robert Fremr (Czech Republic);
- Ms. Taghrid Hikmet (Jordan);
- Ms. Karin Hökborg (Sweden);
- Mr. Vagn Joensen (Denmark);
- Mr. Gberdao Gustave Kam (Burkina Faso);
- Ms. Flavia Lattanzi (Italy);
- Mr. Kenneth Machin (United Kingdom);
- Mr. Joseph Edward Chiondo Masanche (United Republic of Tanzania);
- Mr. Tan Sri Dato' Hj. Mohd. Azmi Dato' Hj. Kamaruddin (Malaysia);
- Mr. Lee Gacuiga Muthoga (Kenya);
- Mr. Seon Ki Park (Republic of Korea);
- Mr. Mparany Mamy Richard Rajohnson (Madagascar);
- Mr. Emile Francis Short (Ghana);
- Mr. Albertus Henricus Johannes Swart (Netherlands);
- Ms. Aura E. Guerra de Villalaz (Panama).

2. *Decides* in response to the request by the Secretary-General to allow ad litem Judges Bossa, Arrey, Lattanzi, Muthoga, Short, Hökborg, Hikmet, Kam and Park to serve in the International Tribunal for Rwanda beyond the cumulative period of service provided for under Article 12 ter of the Statute and until 31 December 2008;

3. *Requests* States to continue to make every effort to ensure that their nationals who were elected as ad litem judges of the International Tribunal for Rwanda remain available to serve until 31 December 2008;
4. *Decides* to remain seized of the matter.

United Nations
S/RES/955 (1994)
8 November 1994

RESOLUTION 955 (1994)

Adopted by the Security Council at its 3453rd meeting, on 8 November 1994

The Security Council, Reaffirming all its previous resolutions on the situation in Rwanda,

Having considered the reports of the Secretary-General pursuant to paragraph 3 of resolution 935 (1994) of 1 July 1994 (S/1994/879 and S/1994/906), and *having taken note* of the reports of the Special Rapporteur for Rwanda of the United Nations Commission on Human Rights (S/1994/1157, annex I and annex II),

Expressing appreciation for the work of the Commission of Experts established pursuant to resolution 935 (1994), in particular its preliminary report on violations of international humanitarian law in Rwanda transmitted by the Secretary-General's letter of 1 October 1994 (S/1994/1125),

Expressing once again its grave concern at the reports indicating that genocide and other systematic, widespread and flagrant violations of international humanitarian law have been committed in Rwanda,

Determining that this situation continues to constitute a threat to international peace and security,

Determined to put an end to such crimes and to take effective measures to bring to justice the persons who are responsible for them,

Convinced that in the particular circumstances of Rwanda, the prosecution of persons responsible for serious violations of international humanitarian law would enable this aim to be achieved and would contribute to the process of national reconciliation and to the restoration and maintenance of peace,

Believing that the establishment of an international tribunal for the prosecution of persons responsible for genocide and the other above-mentioned violations of international humanitarian law will contribute to ensuring that such violations are halted and effectively redressed,

Stressing also the need for international cooperation to strengthen the courts and judicial system of Rwanda, having regard in particular to the necessity for those courts to deal with large numbers of suspects,

Considering that the Commission of Experts established pursuant to resolution 935 (1994) should continue on an urgent basis the collection of information relating to evidence of grave violations of international humanitarian law committed in the territory of Rwanda and should submit its final report to the Secretary-General by 30 November 1994,

Acting under Chapter VII of the Charter of the United Nations,

1. *Decides* hereby, having received the request of the Government of Rwanda (S/1994/1115), to establish an international tribunal for the sole purpose of prosecuting persons responsible for genocide and other serious violations of international humanitarian law committed in the territory of Rwanda and Rwandan citizens responsible for genocide and other such violations committed in the territory of neighbouring States, between 1 January 1994 and 31 December 1994 and to this end to adopt the Statute of the International Criminal Tribunal for Rwanda annexed hereto;
2. *Decides* that all States shall cooperate fully with the International Tribunal and its organs in accordance with the present resolution and the Statute of the International Tribunal and that consequently all States shall take any measures necessary under their domestic law to implement the provisions of the present resolution and the Statute, including the obligation of States to comply with requests for assistance or orders issued by a Trial Chamber under Article 28 of the Statute, and *requests* States to keep the Secretary-General informed of such measures;
3. *Considers* that the Government of Rwanda should be notified prior to the taking of decisions under articles 26 and 27 of the Statute;
4. *Urges* States and intergovernmental and non-governmental organizations to contribute funds, equipment and services to the International Tribunal, including the offer of expert personnel;
5. *Requests* the Secretary-General to implement this resolution urgently and in particular to make practical arrangements for the effective functioning of the International Tribunal, including recommendations to the Council as to possible locations for the seat of the International Tribunal at the earliest time and to report periodically to the Council;
6. *Decides* that the seat of the International Tribunal shall be determined by the Council having regard to considerations of justice and fairness as well as administrative efficiency, including access to witnesses, and economy, and subject to the conclusion of appropriate arrangements between the United Nations and the State of the seat, acceptable to

the Council, having regard to the fact that the International Tribunal may meet away from its seat when it considers it necessary for the efficient exercise of its functions; and *decides* that an office will be established and proceedings will be conducted in Rwanda, where feasible and appropriate, subject to the conclusion of similar appropriate arrangements;

7. *Decides* to consider increasing the number of judges and Trial Chambers of the International Tribunal if it becomes necessary;
8. *Decides* to remain actively seized of the matter.

Annex
Statute of the International Tribunal for Rwanda

Having been established by the Security Council acting under Chapter VII of the Charter of the United Nations, the International Criminal Tribunal for the Prosecution of Persons Responsible for Genocide and Other Serious Violations of International Humanitarian Law Committed in the Territory of Rwanda and Rwandan citizens responsible for genocide and other such violations committed in the territory of neighbouring States, between 1 January 1994 and 31 December 1994 (hereinafter referred to as "the International Tribunal for Rwanda") shall function in accordance with the provisions of the present Statute.

Article 1
Competence of the International Tribunal for Rwanda

The International Tribunal for Rwanda shall have the power to prosecute persons responsible for serious violations of international humanitarian law committed in the territory of Rwanda and Rwandan citizens responsible for such violations committed in the territory of neighbouring States, between 1 January 1994 and 31 December 1994, in accordance with the provisions of the present Statute.

Article 2
Genocide

1. The International Tribunal for Rwanda shall have the power to prosecute persons committing genocide as defined in paragraph 2 of this article or of committing any of the other acts enumerated in paragraph 3 of this article.

2. Genocide means any of the following acts committed with intent to destroy, in whole or in part, a national, ethnical, racial or religious group, as such:

   (a) Killing members of the group;
   (b) Causing serious bodily or mental harm to members of the group;
   (c) Deliberately inflicting on the group conditions of life calculated to bring about its physical destruction in whole or in part;
   (d) Imposing measures intended to prevent births within the group;
   (e) Forcibly transferring children of the group to another group.

3. The following acts shall be punishable:

   (a) Genocide;
   (b) Conspiracy to commit genocide;
   (c) Direct and public incitement to commit genocide;
   (d) Attempt to commit genocide;
   (e) Complicity in genocide.

Article 3
Crimes against humanity

The International Tribunal for Rwanda shall have the power to prosecute persons responsible for the following crimes when committed as part of a widespread or systematic attack against any civilian population on national, political, ethnic, racial or religious grounds:
(a) Murder;
(b) Extermination;
(c) Enslavement;
(d) Deportation;
(e) Imprisonment;
(f) Torture;
(g) Rape;
(h) Persecutions on political, racial and religious grounds;
(i) Other inhumane acts.

Article 4
Violations of Article 3 common to the Geneva Conventions and of Additional Protocol II

The International Tribunal for Rwanda shall have the power to prosecute persons committing or ordering to be committed serious violations of

Article 3 common to the Geneva Conventions of 12 August 1949 for the Protection of War Victims, and of Additional Protocol II thereto of 8 June 1977. These violations shall include, but shall not be limited to:

(a) Violence to life, health and physical or mental well-being of persons, in particular murder as well as cruel treatment such as torture, mutilation or any form of corporal punishment;
(b) Collective punishments;
(c) Taking of hostages;
(d) Acts of terrorism;
(e) Outrages upon personal dignity, in particular humiliating and degrading treatment, rape, enforced prostitution and any form of indecent assault;
(f) Pillage;
(g) The passing of sentences and the carrying out of executions without previous judgement pronounced by a regularly constituted court, affording all the judicial guarantees which are recognized as indispensable by civilized peoples;
(h) Threats to commit any of the foregoing acts.

Article 5
Personal jurisdiction

The International Tribunal for Rwanda shall have jurisdiction over natural persons pursuant to the provisions of the present Statute.

Article 6
Individual criminal responsibility

1. A person who planned, instigated, ordered, committed or otherwise aided and abetted in the planning, preparation or execution of a crime referred to in articles 2 to 4 of the present Statute, shall be individually responsible for the crime.
2. The official position of any accused person, whether as Head of State or Government or as a responsible Government official, shall not relieve such person of criminal responsibility nor mitigate punishment.
3. The fact that any of the acts referred to in articles 2 to 4 of the present Statute was committed by a subordinate does not relieve his or her superior of criminal responsibility if he or she knew or had reason to know that the subordinate was about to commit such acts or had done so and the superior failed to take the necessary and reasonable measures to prevent such acts or to punish the perpetrators thereof.

4. The fact that an accused person acted pursuant to an order of a Government or of a superior shall not relieve him or her of criminal responsibility, but may be considered in mitigation of punishment if the International Tribunal for Rwanda determines that justice so requires.

Article 7
Territorial and temporal jurisdiction

The territorial jurisdiction of the International Tribunal for Rwanda shall extend to the territory of Rwanda including its land surface and airspace as well as to the territory of neighbouring States in respect of serious violations of international humanitarian law committed by Rwandan citizens. The temporal jurisdiction of the International Tribunal for Rwanda shall extend to a period beginning on 1 January 1994 and ending on 31 December 1994.

Article 8
Concurrent jurisdiction

1. The International Tribunal for Rwanda and national courts shall have concurrent jurisdiction to prosecute persons for serious violations of international humanitarian law committed in the territory of Rwanda and Rwandan citizens for such violations committed in the territory of neighbouring States, between 1 January 1994 and 31 December 1994.
2. The International Tribunal for Rwanda shall have primacy over the national courts of all States. At any stage of the procedure, the International Tribunal for Rwanda may formally request national courts to defer to its competence in accordance with the present Statute and the Rules of Procedure and Evidence of the International Tribunal for Rwanda.

Article 9
Non bis in idem

1. No person shall be tried before a national court for acts constituting serious violations of international humanitarian law under the present Statute, for which he or she has already been tried by the International Tribunal for Rwanda.

2. A person who has been tried by a national court for acts constituting serious violations of international humanitarian law may be subsequently tried by the International Tribunal for Rwanda only if:

   (a) The act for which he or she was tried was characterized as an ordinary crime; or
   (b) The national court proceedings were not impartial or independent, were designed to shield the accused from international criminal responsibility, or the case was not diligently prosecuted.

3. In considering the penalty to be imposed on a person convicted of a crime under the present Statute, the International Tribunal for Rwanda shall take into account the extent to which any penalty imposed by a national court on the same person for the same act has already been served.

Article 10
Organization of the International Tribunal for Rwanda

The International Tribunal for Rwanda shall consist of the following organs:
(a) The Chambers, comprising two Trial Chambers and an Appeals Chamber;
(b) The Prosecutor; and
(c) A Registry.

Article 11
Composition of the Chambers

The Chambers shall be composed of eleven independent judges, no two of whom may be nationals of the same State, who shall serve as follows:
(a) Three judges shall serve in each of the Trial Chambers;
(b) Five judges shall serve in the Appeals Chamber.

Article 12
Qualification and election of judges

1. The judges shall be persons of high moral character, impartiality and integrity who possess the qualifications required in their respective countries for appointment to the highest judicial offices. In the overall composition of the Chambers due account shall be taken of the

experience of the judges in criminal law, international law, including international humanitarian law and human rights law.

2. The members of the Appeals Chamber of the International Tribunal for the Prosecution of Persons Responsible for Serious Violations of International Law Committed in the Territory of the Former Yugoslavia since 1991 (hereinafter referred to as "the International Tribunal for the Former Yugoslavia") shall also serve as the members of the Appeals Chamber of the International Tribunal for Rwanda.
3. The judges of the Trial Chambers of the International Tribunal for Rwanda shall be elected by the General Assembly from a list submitted by the Security Council, in the following manner:

   (a) The Secretary-General shall invite nominations for judges of the Trial Chambers from States Members of the United Nations and non-member States maintaining permanent observer missions at United Nations Headquarters;
   (b) Within thirty days of the date of the invitation of the Secretary-General, each State may nominate up to two candidates meeting the qualifications set out in paragraph 1 above, no two of whom shall be of the same nationality and neither of whom shall be of the same nationality as any judge on the Appeals Chamber;
   (c) The Secretary-General shall forward the nominations received to the Security Council. From the nominations received the Security Council shall establish a list of not less than twelve and not more than eighteen candidates, taking due account of adequate representation on the International Tribunal for Rwanda of the principal legal systems of the world;
   (d) The President of the Security Council shall transmit the list of candidates to the President of the General Assembly. From that list the General Assembly shall elect the six judges of the Trial Chambers. The candidates who receive an absolute majority of the votes of the States Members of the United Nations and of the non-Member States maintaining permanent observer missions at United Nations Headquarters, shall be declared elected. Should two candidates of the same nationality obtain the required majority vote, the one who received the higher number of votes shall be considered elected.

4. In the event of a vacancy in the Trial Chambers, after consultation with the Presidents of the Security Council and of the General Assembly, the Secretary-General shall appoint a person meeting the qualifications of paragraph 1 above, for the remainder of the term of office concerned.

5. The judges of the Trial Chambers shall be elected for a term of four years. The terms and conditions of service shall be those of the judges of the International Tribunal for the Former Yugoslavia. They shall be eligible for re-election.

Article 13
Officers and members of the Chambers

1. The judges of the International Tribunal for Rwanda shall elect a President.
2. After consultation with the judges of the International Tribunal for Rwanda, the President shall assign the judges to the Trial Chambers. A judge shall serve only in the Chamber to which he or she was assigned.
3. The judges of each Trial Chamber shall elect a Presiding Judge, who shall conduct all of the proceedings of that Trial Chamber as a whole.

Article 14
Rules of procedure and evidence

The judges of the International Tribunal for Rwanda shall adopt, for the purpose of proceedings before the International Tribunal for Rwanda, the rules of procedure and evidence for the conduct of the pre-trial phase of the proceedings, trials and appeals, the admission of evidence, the protection of victims and witnesses and other appropriate matters of the International Tribunal for the Former Yugoslavia with such changes as they deem necessary.

Article 15
The Prosecutor

1. The Prosecutor shall be responsible for the investigation and prosecution of persons responsible for serious violations of international humanitarian law committed in the territory of Rwanda and Rwandan citizens responsible for such violations committed in the territory of neighbouring States, between 1 January 1994 and 31 December 1994.
2. The Prosecutor shall act independently as a separate organ of the International Tribunal for Rwanda. He or she shall not seek or receive instructions from any Government or from any other source.
3. The Prosecutor of the International Tribunal for the Former Yugoslavia shall also serve as the Prosecutor of the International Tribunal for Rwanda. He or she shall have additional staff, including an additional

Deputy Prosecutor, to assist with prosecutions before the International Tribunal for Rwanda. Such staff shall be appointed by the Secretary-General on the recommendation of the Prosecutor.

Article 16
The Registry

1. The Registry shall be responsible for the administration and servicing of the International Tribunal for Rwanda.
2. The Registry shall consist of a Registrar and such other staff as may be required.
3. The Registrar shall be appointed by the Secretary-General after consultation with the President of the International Tribunal for Rwanda. He or she shall serve for a four- year term and be eligible for reappointment. The terms and conditions of service of the Registrar shall be those of an Assistant Secretary-General of the United Nations.
4. The staff of the Registry shall be appointed by the Secretary-General on the recommendation of the Registrar.

Article 17
Investigation and preparation of indictment

1. The Prosecutor shall initiate investigations ex-officio or on the basis of information obtained from any source, particularly from Governments, United Nations organs, intergovernmental and non-governmental organizations. The Prosecutor shall assess the information received or obtained and decide whether there is sufficient basis to proceed.
2. The Prosecutor shall have the power to question suspects, victims and witnesses, to collect evidence and to conduct on-site investigations. In carrying out these tasks, the Prosecutor may, as appropriate, seek the assistance of the State authorities concerned.
3. If questioned, the suspect shall be entitled to be assisted by counsel of his or her own choice, including the right to have legal assistance assigned to the suspect without payment by him or her in any such case if he or she does not have sufficient means to pay for it, as well as to necessary translation into and from a language he or she speaks and understands.
4. Upon a determination that a prima facie case exists, the Prosecutor shall prepare an indictment containing a concise statement of the facts and the crime or crimes with which the accused is charged under the

Statute. The indictment shall be transmitted to a judge of the Trial Chamber.

Article 18
Review of the indictment

1. The judge of the Trial Chamber to whom the indictment has been transmitted shall review it. If satisfied that a prima facie case has been established by the Prosecutor, he or she shall confirm the indictment. If not so satisfied, the indictment shall be dismissed.
2. Upon confirmation of an indictment, the judge may, at the request of the Prosecutor, issue such orders and warrants for the arrest, detention, surrender or transfer of persons, and any other orders as may be required for the conduct of the trial.

Article 19
Commencement and conduct of trial proceedings

1. The Trial Chambers shall ensure that a trial is fair and expeditious and that proceedings are conducted in accordance with the rules of procedure and evidence, with full respect for the rights of the accused and due regard for the protection of victims and witnesses.
2. A person against whom an indictment has been confirmed shall, pursuant to an order or an arrest warrant of the International Tribunal for Rwanda, be taken into custody, immediately informed of the charges against him or her and transferred to the International Tribunal for Rwanda.
3. The Trial Chamber shall read the indictment, satisfy itself that the rights of the accused are respected, confirm that the accused understands the indictment, and instruct the accused to enter a plea. The Trial Chamber shall then set the date for trial.
4. The hearings shall be public unless the Trial Chamber decides to close the proceedings in accordance with its rules of procedure and evidence.

Article 20
Rights of the accused

1. All persons shall be equal before the International Tribunal for Rwanda.

2. In the determination of charges against him or her, the accused shall be entitled to a fair and public hearing, subject to article 21 of the Statute.
3. The accused shall be presumed innocent until proved guilty according to the provisions of the present Statute.
4. In the determination of any charge against the accused pursuant to the present Statute, the accused shall be entitled to the following minimum guarantees, in full equality:

   (a) To be informed promptly and in detail in a language which he or she understands of the nature and cause of the charge against him or her;
   (b) To have adequate time and facilities for the preparation of his or her defence and to communicate with counsel of his or her own choosing;
   (c) To be tried without undue delay;
   (d) To be tried in his or her presence, and to defend himself or herself in person or through legal assistance of his or her own choosing; to be informed, if he or she does not have legal assistance, of this right; and to have legal assistance assigned to him or her, in any case where the interests of justice so require, and without payment by him or her in any such case if he or she does not have sufficient means to pay for it;
   (e) To examine, or have examined, the witnesses against him or her and to obtain the attendance and examination of witnesses on his or her behalf under the same conditions as witnesses against him or her;
   (f) To have the free assistance of an interpreter if he or she cannot understand or speak the language used in the International Tribunal for Rwanda;
   (g) Not to be compelled to testify against himself or herself or to confess guilt.

Article 21
Protection of victims and witnesses

The International Tribunal for Rwanda shall provide in its rules of procedure and evidence for the protection of victims and witnesses. Such protection measures shall include, but shall not be limited to, the conduct of in camera proceedings and the protection of the victim's identity.

Article 22
Judgement

1. The Trial Chambers shall pronounce judgements and impose sentences and penalties on persons convicted of serious violations of international humanitarian law.
2. The judgement shall be rendered by a majority of the judges of the Trial Chamber, and shall be delivered by the Trial Chamber in public. It shall be accompanied by a reasoned opinion in writing, to which separate or dissenting opinions may be appended.

Article 23
Penalties

1. The penalty imposed by the Trial Chamber shall be limited to imprisonment. In determining the terms of imprisonment, the Trial Chambers shall have recourse to the general practice regarding prison sentences in the courts of Rwanda.
2. In imposing the sentences, the Trial Chambers should take into account such factors as the gravity of the offence and the individual circumstances of the convicted person.
3. In addition to imprisonment, the Trial Chambers may order the return of any property and proceeds acquired by criminal conduct, including by means of duress, to their rightful owners.

Article 24
Appellate proceedings

1. The Appeals Chamber shall hear appeals from persons convicted by the Trial Chambers or from the Prosecutor on the following grounds:

   (a) An error on a question of law invalidating the decision; or
   (b) An error of fact which has occasioned a miscarriage of justice.

2. The Appeals Chamber may affirm, reverse or revise the decisions taken by the Trial Chambers.

Article 25
Review proceedings

Where ao new fact has been discovered which was not known at the time of the proceedings before the Trial Chambers or the Appeals Chamber and which could have been a decisive factor in reaching the decision, the convicted person or the Prosecutor may submit to the International Tribunal for Rwanda an application for review of the judgement.

Article 26
Enforcement of sentences

Imprisonment shall be served in Rwanda or any of the States on a list of States which have indicated to the Security Council their willingness to accept convicted persons, as designated by the International Tribunal for Rwanda. Such imprisonment shall be in accordance with the applicable law of the State concerned, subject to the supervision of the International Tribunal for Rwanda.

Article 27
Pardon or commutation of sentences

If, pursuant to the applicable law of the State in which the convicted person is imprisoned, he or she is eligible for pardon or commutation of sentence, the State concerned shall notify the International Tribunal for Rwanda accordingly. There shall only be pardon or commutation of sentence if the President of the International Tribunal for Rwanda, in consultation with the judges, so decides on the basis of the interests of justice and the general principles of law.

Article 28
Cooperation and judicial assistance

1. States shall cooperate with the International Tribunal for Rwanda in the investigation and prosecution of persons accused of committing serious violations of international humanitarian law.
2. States shall comply without undue delay with any request for assistance or an order issued by a Trial Chamber, including, but not limited to:

   (a) The identification and location of persons;
   (b) The taking of testimony and the production of evidence;
   (c) The service of documents;
   (d) The arrest or detention of persons;
   (e) The surrender or the transfer of the accused to the International Tribunal for Rwanda.

Article 29
The status, privileges and immunities of the International Tribunal for Rwanda

1. The Convention on the Privileges and Immunities of the United Nations of 13 February 1946 shall apply to the International Tribunal for Rwanda, the judges, the Prosecutor and his or her staff, and the Registrar and his or her staff.
2. The judges, the Prosecutor and the Registrar shall enjoy the privileges and immunities, exemptions and facilities accorded to diplomatic envoys, in accordance with international law.
3. The staff of the Prosecutor and of the Registrar shall enjoy the privileges and immunities accorded to officials of the United Nations under articles V and VII of the Convention referred to in paragraph 1 of this article.
4. Other persons, including the accused, required at the seat or meeting place of the International Tribunal for Rwanda shall be accorded such treatment as is necessary for the proper functioning of the International Tribunal for Rwanda.

Article 30
Expenses of the International Tribunal for Rwanda

The expenses of the International Tribunal for Rwanda shall be expenses of the Organization in accordance with Article 17 of the Charter of the United Nations.

Article 31
Working languages

The working languages of the International Tribunal shall be English and French.

Article 32
Annual report

The President of the International Tribunal for Rwanda shall submit an annual report of the International Tribunal for Rwanda to the Security Council and to the General Assembly.

Appendix II

Key Indicators of the Rwandan Vision 2020

Indicators	Situation In 2000	Target in 2010	Target in 2020	International level
1. Rwandan population	7,700,000	10,200,000	13,000,000	
2. Literacy level	48	80	100	100
3. Life expectancy (years)	49	50	55	
4. Women fertility rate	6.5	5.5	4.5	
5. Infant mortality rate (0/00)	107	80	50	
6. Maternal mortality rate (0/00.000)	1070	600	200	
7. Child malnutrition (Insufficiency in %)	30	20	10	
8. Population growth rate (%)	2.9	2.3	2.2	
9. Net primary school enrollment (%)	72	100	100	100
10. Growth secondary school enrollment (%)	100	100		
11. Secondary school transitional rate (%)	42	60	80	
12. Growth secondary school enrollment (%)	7	40	60	
13. Rate of qualification of teachers (%)	20	100	100	100
14. Professional and technical training centers	50	106		
15. The rate of admission in tertiary education (0/00)	1	4	6	
16. Gender equality in tertiary education (%)	30	40	50	50
17. Gender equality in decision-making positions (% of females)	10	30	40	
18. HIV/AIDS prevalence rate (%)	13	11	8	0
19. Malaria-related mortality (%)	51	30	25	
20. Doctors per 100,000 inhabitants	1.5	5	10	10
21. Population in a good hygienic condition (%)	20	40	60	
22. Nurses per 100,000 inhabitants	16	18	20	20
23. Laboratory technicians per 100,000 inhabitants	2	5	5	
24. Poverty (% < $1/day)	64	40	30	

Indicators	Situation In 2000	Target in 2010	Target in 2020	International level
25. Average GDP growth rate (%)	6.2	8	8	
26. Growth rate of the agricultural sector (%)	9	8	6	
27. Growth rate of the industry sector (%)	7	9	12	
28. Growth rate of the service sector (%)	7	9	11	
29. Ginni coefficient (income disparity)	0.454	0.400	0.350	
30. Growth national savings (% of GDP)	1	4	6	
31. Growth national investment (% of GDP)	18	23	30	30
32. GDP per capita in U.S. dollar	220	400	900	
33. Urban population (%)	10	20	30	
34. Agricultural population (%)	90	75	50	
35. Modernized agricultural land (%)	3	20	50	
36. Use of fertilizers (kg/ha/year)	0.5	8	15	
37. Financial credits to the agricultural sector (%)	1	15	20	
38. Access to clear water (%)	52	80	100	100
39. Agricultural production (kcal/day/person; % needs)	1612	2000	2200	
40. Availability of proteins/person/day (% of needs)	35	55	65	70
41. Road network (km/km2)	0.54	0.56	0.60	
42. Annual electricity consumption (kWh/inhabitants)	30	60	100	
43. Access to electric energy (% of population.)	2	25	35	
44. Land portion against soil erosion (%)	20	80	90	
45. Level of reforestation (ha)				
46. Wood energy in the national energy consumption (%)	94	50	50	
47. Nonagricultural jobs	200.000	500.000	1.400.000	

Notes

Preface

1. From a speech delivered at the Development Partners Meeting on November 22, 2006, at the Intercontinental Hotel in Kigali.

Chapter 1

1. See Oscar Kimanuka's article titled "ICT best path to development" printed in the *East African* on May 14–20, 2007.
2. It was Robert McNamara, the WB president, who, in his famous Nairobi speech in 1973, proposed the term "absolute poverty" as a condition of deprivation that "falls below any rational definition of human decency." It applies today to sub-Saharan Africa, where the majority of the population lives on less than one U.S. dollar a day. See http://www.imf.org/external/pubs.
3. See Public Sector Management Reforms in Africa: Lessons Learned, which can be located at http://www.uneca.org/eca_resources/publications.
4. See http://www.uneca.org/eca_resources/publications:dpmd/publicsector.mangt .pdf.
5. Ibid.
6. See http://www.time.com/time/magazine/article.
7. See Public Sector Management Reforms in Africa, in Economic Commission for Africa,http://www.uneca.org/eca_resources/publications/dpmd/public_Sector _mangt.pdf.
8. See http://web.worldbank.org/WEBSITE/EXTERNAL/COUNTRIES/AFRICAEXT/ RWANDAEXTN.
9. See the Ministry of Finance and Economic Planning Poverty Reduction Strategy Annual Progress Report, June 2003–June 2004.
10. Ibid.
11. See http://www.minecofin.co.rw.
12. See the report of the Development Partners Meeting, held on December 1–2, 2005, at the Intercontinental Hotel in Kigali.
13. Ibid.
14. See http://www.minecofin.co.rw.
15. Ibid.

16. See Rwanda's Vision 2020 document, available at http://www.minecofin.co.rw.
17. See the South African Minister of Public Service and Administration's speech delivered on December 12, 2005, available at http://www.african-union.org/Politicalaffairs.
18. See Rawi M. Tawfik's "Nepad and African Development: Towards a New Partnership between Development Actors in Africa."

Chapter 2

1. See Pricewaterhouse Cooper's (2003, 10) draft report, Public Sector Reform: Towards a Future Strategic Framework, presented to the government of Ghana.
2. See the report on a meeting of Donor Public Service Reform Working Groups held in London on April 22–23, 2002, available at http://www.adb.org/wgpsr/Draft_Report.
3. See Professor Apollo Nsibambi's speech delivered on June 23, 2005, at the Uganda Management Institute to mark the Africa Day of Administration and Civil Service and the United Nations Public Service Day.
4. Ibid.
5. See "Civil Service Reform: The True Impact of Retrenchment" in the September 1997 *Insights* issue no. 23.
6. Ibid.
7. Ibid.
8. Ibid.
9. See D. K. Kalinaki, in the East African, May 14–20, 2007; in www.nationmedia.com; p.9
10. Ibid.
11. See the report on a meeting of the Donor Public Service Reform Working Group held in London on April 22–23, 2002, available at http://www.adb.org/wgpsrt/Draft_report.
12. See "Applying the Rapid Results Approach in Kenya," available at http://web.worldbank.org.
13. See "Kenya: A worthy civil service goal," printed in the *Nation* newspaper on June 9, 2006.
14. See "Kibaki upbeat on economic reforms," printed in *The Standard* newspaper on September 20, 2006, which can be accessed at http://www.eastandard.net/htm_news/news.
15. See http://www.independent.co.uk/news/business/analysis-and-features/kenya's economy-in-crisis.
16. This is an economy in which production levels and prices are controlled by some central authority. This contrasts with a free market economy. Socialist (or communist) economies are generally command economies, and they have been shown to fail. See http://bonivation.com/cbs/commandEconomy.jsp.

17. As cited in Danielson (2001), this differed from established posts, which had to be approved centrally by the Public Service Commission and the Department of Human Resource Management and Development to create the so-called ghost workers, nonexistent employees whose salaries were pocketed by rackets led by senior civil servants.
18. See C. P. Msosa, director of Management Services, Office of the President and Cabinet of Malawi in www.tanzania.gov.tz/psrp/malawi.htm.
19. See http://www.tanzania.gov.tz/psrp/malawi.htm.
20. Ibid.
21. See the government of Malawi's September 1996 action plan for civil service reform.
22. It should, however, be observed that the correlation between aid per capita and income per capita is less than perfect. The poorest members of the union do not receive more aid per capita than the relatively richer members.
23. Op Cit.
24. See the CIA World Factbook at http://www.cia.gov/publications.
25. See the U.S. Department of State at http://www.state.gov.
26. Ibid.
27. This policy refers to the gradual dismantling of state controls built up from the late 1960s.
28. Op Cit.
29. See also Botchery et al. 1998.
30. Op Cit.
31. According to Lienert and Modi (1997), although reduction in the statutory retirement age may have an impact on the size of the civil service workforce, it does not necessarily improve government finances because of both higher pensions and smaller employee contributions.
32. See the CIA World Factbook at http://www.cia.gov/publications.
33. The Millennium Challenge Account (MCA) is administered by a government corporation in the United States and is designed to support innovative strategies and ensure accountability for measurable results. It rewards countries "that root out corruption, respect human rights, and adhere to the rule of law . . . invest in better healthcare, better schools and broader immunization and have more open markets and sustainable budget policies, nations where people can start and operate a small business without running the gauntlet of bureaucracy and bribery," as stated in a speech by President George W. Bush on March 22, 2002, which can be found at http://www.whitehouse.org.
34. Op Cit, p.182.

Chapter 3

1. "Rwanda remembered." *The Economist*, March 2004.
2. IMF's paper titled "Rwanda-Enhanced Structural Adjustment Facility Economic and Financial Policy Framework Paper for 1998/99–2000/01, accessed at http://www.imf.org/external/np/pfp/rwanda.

3. United Nations General Assembly at its fiftieth session on October 19, 1995.
4. See the World Bank, "Rwandese Republic Emergency Recovery Project Technical Annex," accessed at http://www.um.dk/publikationer/Danida/English.
5. See http://www.dfidrwanda.org/page.htm, accessed August 13, 2006.
6. The release from the DFID office is quoted in Kigali's daily *New Times* issue of July 23, 2006.
7. See government of Rwanda integrated socioeconomic and ICT policy and strategies for accelerated development, February, 2000.
8. See IMF press release 06/121, June 8, 2006.
9. The National Unity and Reconciliation Commission was created by Law No. 03/99 on March 12, 1999.
10. Remarks by Augustin Carstens, deputy managing director of the IMF on June 7, 2006, at the IMF offices in Washington D.C.
11. The report was launched on July 15, 2004, at the India Habitat Center in New Delhi.
12. From a speech delivered by His Excellency President Paul Kagame at California State University, Sacramento, on April 14, 2005, on the topic of managing ethnic relations and national reconciliation in post-genocide Rwanda.
13. Mamdani, M. 2001. *When victims became killers: Colonialism, nativism and the genocide in Rwanda*. Princeton University Press.
14. This is contained in an interview granted by Mr. Gerard Niyitegeka, Rwanda's Central Bank governor in May 1995, with ReliefWeb. See http://www.reliefweb.int/library/nordic/book4.
15. See Government of Rwanda, Document Cadre pour la Réhabilitation et le Renforcement d'Urgence des Capacités des Gestion Economique.
16. See National Strategy Framework Paper on Strengthening Good Governance for Poverty Reduction in Rwanda, March 2002.
17. PRSP has been renamed Economic Development for Poverty Reduction Strategy (EDPRS).
18. See http://dsp-psd.pwgsc.ca/collection/CD4, accessed August 5, 2006.
19. Calestous Juma is a professor of international development at Harvard University.
20. See http://www.minaloc.gov.rw/good_governance/national.
21. See MINALOC's National Decentralisation Policy at http://www.minaloc.gov.rw/doc/policy.
22. See the Swedish International Development Agency (SIDA) Evaluation 04/33, accessed at http://www.sida.se/publication.
23. See Anne Louise Grinsted (ODI-Fellow), Fiscal Decentralisation in Rwanda, accessed at: http: www.geppa.dk/files/activities.
24. See MINALOC: Fiscal Decentralisation in Rwanda, accessed at http://www.geppa.dk/files/activities/fiscal.
25. Ibid.
26. See the seminar on Fiscal Decentralisation, January 12, 2006, syllabus accessed at http://www.geppa.dk/files.
27. Ibid.

28. See MINALOC: Five Years of Decentralization Implementation Program (DIP).
29. Ibid.
30. Ibid.
31. See MINALOC presents accountability on reforms; *New Times*, http://www.minaloc.gov.rw/spip.php?article49.
32. Ibid.
33. These are the president, speakers of the senate, lower chamber of deputies, the prime minister and the chief justice. See cabinet proceedings of February 3, 2005, and http://www.gov.rw.
34. Monitor. See http://www.monotor.co.ug.
35. See Sunika, Kikeri, and Aishetu Kolo (2006) State Enterprises. See http://rru.worldbank.org.
36. Kabango, Vianney: Privatisation in Rwanda: Is it eggs going bad?; Kigali, September, 2006, The New Times, Newspaper, www.newtimes.co.rw.
37. Ibid.
38. Rwanda National Privatization Secretariat, http://www.minaloc.gov.rw/spip.php?/decentralisation.
39. See the November 12, 2006 edition of the *New Times*, accessed at http://www.newtimes.co.rw.

Chapter 4

1. Vision 2020: Rwanda's struggle for prosperity. *New Times*, January 30, 2006.
2. Ibid.
3. Accessed at: http://www.usaid.gov/pubs.
4. Accessed at: http://www.newtimes.co.rw, article by James Karuhanga and Kennedy Ndahiro, "Rwandans Vote," September 16, 2008.
5. Accessed the *New Times* at http://www.newtimes.co.rw, article by James Karuhanga and Kennedy Ndahiro, "Rwanda: Citizen's vote," September 17, 2008, 3.
6. The WB's Rwanda background paper for the Donor Meeting on budget financing held in Paris, France, on July 24, 1997.
7. The IMF and the IDA report on Rwanda, March, 27, 2006, accessed at http://www.worldbank.org/resources/Rwanda.
8. The Joint Staff Advisory Note of the Poverty Reduction Paper Annual Progress Report by the World Bank and the IMF, approved by Sharmini Coorey and Mark Plant on March 27, 2006.
9. Ibid.
10. Economic Commission for Africa. 2004. Public Sector Management Reforms in Africa: Lessons Learned; Development Policy Management Division. Addis Ababa: African Union.
11. Vanessa Harrhoff, in Rwanda Funds ICT development, in www.itweb.co.za.
12. A Government of Rwanda (GOR) policy document for the realization of the vision for Rwanda—to transform the country into an information-rich knowledge-based society and economy within twenty years. Government of

Rwanda policy document, February 2000. Accessed at http://www.uneca.org/aisi/NICI/country_profiles/rwanda.

13. Ibid.
14. Ibid.
15. RITA; A Review of the Implementation of the Rwanda ICT4/NICI 2005 Plan, p.
16. Suuna, Ignatius. Appraisal in ministries underway. *New Times*, August 29, 2006. http://www.newtimes.co.rw.
17. Mukombozi, Robert, and Berna Namata. "President's office sermons government planners." *New Times*. August 25, 2006.

Chapter 5

1. Mawutodzi K. Abissath, 2008, "African ICT Gurus, where are you?"; accessed at http://wwwghana.gov.gh/dexadd/feature/ict_gurus.pdf.
2. Albert Butare, minister of state in charge of telecommunications and energy, interviewed in an article by Magnus K.Mazimpaka, which appeared in the *New Times* on April 25, 2007.
3. Canadian International Development Agency; accessed at http://www.acdi-gc.ca.
4. Rita is the Rwanda Information and Telecommunications Agency and has the mission to lead the process of creating the Rwanda Information Society and developing the economy in line with the aspirations of the country's vision. It was created in 2002 by an act of parliament. This act was revised and approved by the Rwandan parliament in October 2006. Accessed at: http://www.rita.rw/ See http://rw.
5. Rwanda's Vision 2020 is a framework for Rwanda's development, presenting the key priorities and providing Rwandans with a guiding tool for the future. Accessed at: http://moh.gov.rw/docs/vision2020.doc.
6. Building Science, Technology and Innovation Capacity in Rwanda, World Bank, 2008, p.ix.
7. Vision 2020 is a framework for Rwanda's development, presenting the key priorities and providing Rwandans with a guiding tool for the future. It supports a clear Rwandan identity, whilst showing ambition and imagination in overcoming poverty and division. The Rwandan Government, together with its partners, donors, civil society organizations and the private sector, is now in the process of formulating more detailed sectoral plans in order to attain the goals of Vision 2020.
8. Andrew Mack and Jeremy Goldwater. "Rwanda's knowledge Revolution: Technology and Telecoms," *Business in Africa*, March 1, 2007.
9. *New Times article dated* October 30, 2007, on the Kigali ICT Summit held at the Kigali Serena Hotel; accessed at: http://see www.newtimes.co.rw.
10. Ibid.
11. http://www.nepad.gov.rw.
12. http://www.newtimes.co.rw.

13. NEPAD Secretariat. 2007. Use of Computers and Internet amongst boys and girls. Office of the President Rwanda. www.nepad.co.rw.
14. Kagame Paul, 2007, speech delivered in Addis Ababa, January 2007. Accessed at: http://www.gov.rw.

Chapter 6

1. Peters, Lucien. 1999. Downsizing the civil service in developing countries: Golden handshakes or smiling farewells? Public Administration and development; No.18, 1998, P.381.
2. The South African Institute of International Affairs. See http://www.saiia.org.za.
3. See http://www.wikipedia.org/wiki/Developed_country.
4. Public Sector Reforms in Africa: Lessons Learned, ECA, Addis Ababa, December 2004.
5. Ibid., 44
6. Olowu, D. 2003. Restoring public service leadership in Africa—Moving from tactical to strategic responses: A critical challenge to NEPAD. Netherlands: Institute of Social Studies, the Hague
7. Ibid., 45.
8. Guido, B., and Yolande Jemiai. 2000. Public sector revisited in the context of globalisation. United Nations Department of Economic and Social Affairs. Paper delivered to a seminar on public administration reform in Beijing. July 15.
9. Ibid.
10. Ibid.
11. See http://www.nepad.org.

References

Abdulrahman, Tajudeen. 2007. What is a wolf doing in a bank meant to help the poor? *New Vision* (May 16), http://www.newvision.co.ug/D/8/20/565433.

Abrahamsen, Rita. 2000. *Disciplining democracy: Development discourse and good governance in Africa*. London: Zed Books.

Adamolekun, Ladipo, ed. 2002. *Public administration in Africa: Main issues and selected country studies*. St. Helier, Jersey: Spectrum Books.

Adamolekun, Ladipo, et al. 1997. Political transition, economic liberalization, and civil service reform in Malawi. IDPM Public Policy and Working Paper no 16, University of Manchester, Institute for Development Policy and Management (IDPM).

Adams, A., and T. Harnett. 1996. Cost sharing in the social sectors of sub-Saharan Africa: Impact on the poor. World Bank Discussion Paper, no. 338, Washington, D.C.

African Peer Review Mechanism. 2006. Country review report of the Republic of Rwanda, no. 2. Midrand, South Africa: APRM Secretariat.

Alemika, Etannibi E. O. 1993. Colonialism, state, and policing in Nigeria. *Crime, Law and Social Change* 20 (3): 187–219.

Anwar, Shah, ed. 2005. *Public sector governance and accountability series: Public expenditure analysis*. Washington, D.C.: World Bank.

Aron, J. 1997. Political, economic, and social institutions: A review of growth evidence. CSAE Working Papers 98/4, Centre for the Study of African Economies, Oxford.

Awed, H. 1998. Structural adjustment and gender in sub-Saharan Africa. MA diss., University of Manchester, UK.

Balogun, M. J. 2001. Performance improvement and customer satisfaction a focus of public service reform: Trends and challenges in Africa. *Public Administration Quarterly* 25 (3): 205–15.

Balogun, M. J. 2003. Nigeria's public service reform processes. http://un.org/intradoc/groups.

Banda, B. R. 1996. *Implementing civil service reforms: What Malawi can learn from experiences of other countries*. Birmingham, AL: University of Birmingham Publication.

Bangura, Y. 2000. Public sector restructuring: The institutional and social effects of fiscal, managerial, and capacity building reforms. Paper No. 3, United Nations Research Institute for Social Development.

Bangur Barya, J. J. 1993. The new political conditionalities of aid: An independent view from Africa. *IDS Bulletin* 24 (1): 16–22.

Batley, R. 1999. The new public management in developing countries: Implications for policy and organizational reform. *Journal of International Development* 2 (5): 761–65.

Belshaw, D., and I. Livingstone. 2002. *Renewing development in sub-Saharan Africa: Policy, performance, and prospects*. London: Routledge.

Bigsten, Arne, and Steve Kayizzi-Mugerwa. 2000. The political economy of policy failure. Working Papers in Economics 23, Goteborg University, Department of Economics.

Blunt, P., and M. L. Jones. 1992. *Managing organizations in Africa: Readings, cases, and exercises*. Berlin: Walter de Gruyter.

Brewer, Gene A., and Sally C. Selden. 2000. Why elephants gallop: Assessing and producing organizational performance in federal agencies. *Journal of Public Administration Research and Theories* 10 (4): 685–712.

Buchanan, D., and D. Boddy. 1992. *The expertise of the change agent: Public performance and backstage activity*. UK: Prentice Hall.

Buchanan, D., and A. Huczynski. 1997. *Organizational behaviour: An introductory text*. 3rd ed. New York: Prentice Hall.

Burnes, B. 1996. *Managing change: A strategic approach to organizational dynamics*. 2nd ed. Great Britain: Pitman.

Bush, George. 2002. The Millennium Challenge Account (MCA) speech. March 22. http://www.whitehouse.org.

Butare, Albert. 2007. Minister discussion on telecommunication and energy. *New Times*, April 25.

Byaruahnga, Charles. 2002. *Modernizing government: Integrating structural and budget reforms for a better performing public sector*. London: Adam Smith Institute.

Camdessus, Michelle. 1999. Opening remarks to IMF conference on second generation reforms. November 8. Washington, D.C.

Canadian International Development Agency. 2005. Programming Framework 2005–2011. CIDA. Gatineau. http://www.acdi-cida.gc.ca/CIDAWEB/acdicida.nsf/En/JUD-22212111-MYG.

Carstens, Augustin. 2006. Reshaping the IMF's role in the 21st Century. Presented at the Fifth Annual Regional Conference on Central America, Punta Cana, Dominican Republic, June 29, 2006.

Cohen, J. M. 1993. Importance of public service reform: The case of Kenya. *Journal of Modern African Studies* 31 (3): 449–76.

Common, R. 1998. The new public management and policy transfer: Role of international organizations. In *Beyond the new public management: Changing ideas and practices in government*, ed. M. Minogue, C. Polidano, and D. Hulme. Manchester, UK: Edward Elgar Publishing.

Commonwealth Secretariat. 1997. *Current good practices and new developments in public service management: A profile of the public Service of Zimbabwe*. London: Commonwealth Secretariat.

Cook, P., C. H. Kirkpatrick, and F. I. Nixson, eds. 1998. *Privatization, enterprise development and economic reform: Experiences of developing and transitional economies*. Gloucestershire, UK: Edward Elgar Publishing.

Coolidge, J., and S. Rose-Ackerman. 1997. High level rent seeking and corruption in African regimes: Theory and causes. World Bank Working Paper 1780, World Bank, Washington, D.C.

Cope, S., F. Leishman, and P. Starie. 1997. Globalization, new public management and the enabling state: Futures of police management. *International Journal of Public Sector Management* 10 (6): 444–60.

Curtis, S. 1994. Change: The rocky but rewarding road. In *Managing change in the new public sector*, ed. R. Lovell. London, England: Longman.

Dallaire, Lt. Gen. Romeo. 2003. *Shake hands with the devil: The failure of humanity in Rwanda*. Canada: Randolf.

Danielson, Anders. 2001. Economic and institutional reforms in French speaking West Africa: Impact on efficiency and growth. Discussion Paper 2001/28, University of Lund.

Devereux, Stephen. 2000. Social justice and the distribution of income, Social Policy Conference. Paper presented in Lilongwe, Malawi. Institute for Development Studies. IDS Working Paper No. 216, Sussex, UK.

DFID. 2006. Poverty reduction, budget support to Rwanda, 13 August DFID, Kigali, Rwanda. http://www.dfidrwanda.org/page.html.

———. 2001. DFID departmental report 2001, London: Stationary Office.

Dia, M. 1994. Civil service reform: The African experience. In *Civil service reform in Latin America and the Caribbean: Proceedings of a conference*, ed. S. A. Chaudhry, G. J. Reid, and W. H. Malik. Washington, D.C.: World Bank.

Doe, L. 1998. Civil service reform in the countries of the West African Monetary Union. *International Social Science Journal* 50 (1).

Dolowitz, D. P., and D. Marsh. 1998. Policy transfer: A framework for comparative analysis. In *Beyond the new public management: Changing ideas and practices in government*, ed. M. Minogue, C. Polidano, and D. Hulme. Cheltenham: Edward Elgar Publishing.

Dwivedi, O. P., and J. Nef. 1982. Crises and continuities in development theory and administration: First and Third World perspectives. *Public Administration and Development* 2: 59–77.

Dzidonni, Clement. 2005. Rwanda ICT 4D/NICI-2005 plan: Achievements, lessons and challenges. http://www.iniiti.com.

Economic Commission for Africa. 2005. Governance for a progressing Africa. ECA Addis Ababa. http://www.uneca.org/eca_resources/Publications/index.asp.

———. 2003. Assessing regional integration in Africa. ECA Addis Ababa. http://www.uneca.org/eca_resources/Publications/index.asp.

———. 2003. Public sector reforms in Africa: Lessons learned, May, ECA, Addis Ababa.

Ekeh, Peter P. 1975. Colonialism and the two publics in Africa: A theoretical statement. *Comparative Studies in Society and History* 17: 91–112.

Enos, J. L. 1995. *In pursuit of science and technology in sub-Saharan Africa: The impact of structural adjustment programmes*. London: Routledge.

Farnham, D., and S. Horton. 1993. The new public service managerialism: An assessment. In *Managing the new public services*, ed. D. Farnham and S. Horton. London, England: Macmillan.

Ferlie, E., L. Ashburner, L. Fitzgerald, and A. Pettigrew. 1996. *The new public management in action*. Oxford: Oxford University Press.

Gay, P. 1996. Making up managers: Enterprise and the ethos of bureaucracy. In *Politics of management knowledge*, ed. S. R. Clegg and G. Palmer. London: SAGE.

Government of Rwanda. 2002. National strategy framework paper on strengthening good governance for poverty reduction in Rwanda, March. Kigali, Rwanda: Government of Rwanda.

———. 1999. *National unity and reconciliation commission: Mandate and operations* No. 03/99, March. Kigali, Rwanda: Government of Rwanda.

Gregory, R. J. 1996. Bureaucratic "psychopathology" and technocratic governance: Whiter responsibility? *Hong Kong Public Administration* 4 (1): 17–36.

Grindle, M. S., and J. W. Thomas. 1991. *Public choices and policy change: The political economy of reform in developing countries*. Baltimore, United States: John Hopkins.

Grindle, Merilee. 2003. The good, the bad, and the unavoidable: Improving the public service in poor countries. In *Public Service in 21st Century*, ed. John Donahue and Joseph Nye. Washington, D.C.: Brookings Institute.

Grinsted, Anne Louise. 2004. Fiscal decentralization in Rwanda (ODI-Fellow). http://www.geppa.dk/files/activities.

Grundberg, I. 1998. *World Development Report* 26 (4): 591–605.

Guido, B., and Yolande Jemiai. 2000. Public sector revisited in the context of globalization. Paper delivered to a seminar on public administration reform in Beijing, United Nations Department of Economic and Social Affairs.

Hamdok, Abdalla. 2003. Governance and policy in Africa: Recent experiences. In *Reforming Africa's institutions: Ownership, incentives, and capabilities*, ed. Steve Kayizzi-Mugerwa, 15. New York: United Nations University Press.

Hansen, T. 2005. The Gacaca tribunals in post-genocide Rwanda, November 27. Center for Restorative Justice and Peacemaking. University of Minnesota. http://rjp.umn.edu/img/assets/13522/Gacaca_Tribunals.pdf.

Hawthorn, G. 1993. How to ask for good government. *IDS Bulletin* 24 (1): 24–30.

Heeks, R. 1999. Better information age reform: Reducing the risk of information systems failure. In *Reinventing government in the information age: International practice in IT-enabled public sector reform*, ed. R. Heeks. London: Routledge.

Hood, Christopher. 1991. A public management for all seasons. *Public Administration* 69 (1): 3–19.

Hossam, A. 1998. Structural adjustment and gender in sub-Saharan Africa. PhD diss., University of Manchester, IDPM.

Hussey, D. 1998. *Strategic management: From theory to implementation*. London, Great Britain: Butterworth-Heinemann.

IDA. 1996. Rwanda: Country assessment strategy—Progress report, Washington, D.C. http://www.wds.worldbank.org/..WDSP/IB/1999.

IMF. 2006. IMF executive board completes the sixth review of Rwanda's PRGF arrangement and approves a new three-year PRGF arrangement. http://www.imf.org/external/np/sec/pr/2006/pr06121.htm.

———. 1998. Rwanda: Enhanced structural adjustment facility economic and financial policy framework paper for 1998/99–2000/01. http://www.imf.org/external/np/pfp/rwanda.

Inter Parliamentary Union. 2008. Women in national parliaments. Inter Parliamentary Union, Geneva. http://www.ipu.org.

Kabango, Vianney. 2006. Privatisation in Rwanda: Is it eggs going bad? *New Times*, September. http://www.newtimes.co.rw.

Kagame, Paul. 2005. Managing ethnic relations and national reconciliation in post genocide. Rwanda speech. Sacramento: California State University.

———. 2007. Science, technology, and research for Africa's development. Address to the 8th Summit of African Union on Science and Technology. African Union. Addis Ababa.

Kalinaki, D. K. 2007. The condom debate. *East African Weekly*, May14–20. http://www.nationmedia.com.

Kanyarukiga, Sam, et al. 2005. Evaluation of DFID country programmes for Rwanda. http://www.dfid.gov.uk.

Karen, Attwood. 2008. Kenya's economy in crisis. *Independent Newspaper*, January 25, Business section. http://www.independent.co.uk/news/business/analysis-and-features/kenya's economy-in-crisis.

Katz, Rob, and Andrew Mack. 2007. *Telecommunications and IT*. Washington, D.C.: World Resources Institute.

Kaul, M., and P. Collins. 1995. Governments in transition: Towards a public administration. *Public Administration and Development* 15: 199–206.

Kauzya, J. M. 2003. Public sector reconfiguration and transformation. Strategic paper. Paper presented to the Ministry of Public Service and Labor, Government of Rwanda.

Kayizzi-Mugerwa, Steve. 2003. *Reforming Africa's institutions: Ownership, incentives and capabilities*. New York: United Nations University Press.

Kazooba, C. 2006. Rwanda: Burundi join EAC in March. *New Times*, February 13. http://www.rwandagateway.org/article.php3?id_article=1593.

Kibaki, Mwai. 2006. Upbeat on economic reforms. *Standard*, September 20. http://www.eastandard.net/htm_news/news.

Kiggundu, Moses N. 1997. *Managing globalization in developing countries and transition economies*. Westport, CT: Greenwood Publishing.

Kimanuka, Oscar. 2007. ICT best path to development. *East African (Weekly)*, May 14.

Kiviat, Barbara. 2008. Starbucks looks for a fresh jolt. *Time Magazine*, March 27. http://www.time.com/time/magazine/article/0,9171,1725973,00.html.

Kirkpatrick, C. 1995. Trade Policy Reforms and Performance in Africa in the 1980s: *Journal of Modern African Studies* 33 (2): 285–98.

Klitgaard, R. 1989. Incentive myopia. *World Development* 17(4): 447–59.

Lancaster, C. 1993. Governance and development: The views from Washington. *IDS Bulletin* 24 (1): 9–15.

Larmore, C. 1987. *Patterns of moral complexity*. Cambridge, MA: Cambridge University Press.

Lawrence, Peter. 2002. Structural adjustment and sub-Saharan Africa. In *Handbook on development policy and management*, ed. Colin Kirkpatrick. Cheltenham, UK: Edward Elgar Publishing.

Levy, Brian. 2003. A comparative review of administrative reform in Ghana, Tanzania, and Zambia. Washington, D.C: World Bank.

Lewis, Peter. ed. 1998. *Africa: Dilemmas of development*. Colorado: Westview Press.

Lienert, I. 1998. *Civil service reform in Africa: Mixed results after 10 years: Handbook of public administration*. California: Sage.

Lienert, I., and J. Modi. 1997. A decade of civil service reform in sub-Saharan Africa. IMF Working Paper No. 97/179.

Lovell, R. 1994. Understanding people. In *Managing change in the new public sector*, ed. R. Lovell. Manchester, UK: Longman.

Lucien, P. 1999. Downsizing the civil service in developing countries: Golden handshakes or smiling farewells? *Public Administration and Development* (18).

Lwakabamba, S. 2006. Learning from others. In *The development of ICTs in Rwanda: Pioneering experiences*. Ottawa: IDRC Books.

McCourt, W. 2002. New public management in developing countries. In *New public management: Current trends and future prospects*, ed. K. McLaughlin, S. Osborne, and E. Ferlie, 1–15. London: Routledge.

McHugh, M. 1999. Trouble in paradise: Disintegrated strategic change within a government agency. *International Journal of Public Sector Management* 10 (6): 433–43.

McNamara, Robert. 1973. Records of President Robert S. McNamara's annual meetings speech in Nairobi WB IBRD/IDA 03–04. 1.2.

Mack, Andrew, and Jeremy Goldberg. 2008. Rwanda's knowledge revolution. *Business in Africa*, March 1.

Mamdani, M. 2001. *When victims became killers: Colonialism, nativism and the genocide in Rwanda*. New Jersey: Princeton University Press.

Mawutodzi, Abissath. 2006. African ICT gurus, where are you? Abissath Blog. http://abissathfeatures-mawu.blogspot.com (accessed July 16, 2007).

Merrick, Jones. 2004. Swedish support to decentralization in Rwanda. Swedish International Development Agency SIDA Evaluations, April 33, Stockholm. http://www.sida.se/publications.

Ministry of Finance and Economic Planning. 2006. Economic development and poverty reduction strategy. Kigali, Rwanda: Government of Rwanda. http://www.minecofin.gov.rw/en/inno-read_article.php?articleId=4&highlight=Economic%20reports.

———. 2006. Vision 2020: Rwanda's struggle for prosperity. *New Times*, January 30.

———. 2005. Poverty reduction strategy paper annual progress report. Kigali, Rwanda: Government of Rwanda. http://www.imf.org/external/pubs/ft/scr/2005/cr05127.pdf.

———. 2004. Kigali, Rwanda: Government of Rwanda.

———. 2000. Empowering the private sector. Rwanda National Privatization Secretariat. Kigali, Rwanda.

———. 2000. Rwanda vision 2020. Kigali, Rwanda: Government of Rwanda.

Ministry of ICT. 2000. Integrated socioeconomic and ICT policy and strategies for accelerated development. Kigali, Rwanda: Government of Rwanda.

Ministry of Local Government. 2006. Good governance. National strategy framework paper. Kigali, Rwanda: Government of Rwanda. http://www.minaloc.gov.rw/good_governance/national.

———. 2006. MINALOC Presents accountability on reforms. *New Times*, July 13, News section.

———. 2005. Fiscal decentralization in Rwanda. Kigali, Rwanda: Government of Rwanda. http://www.geppa.dk/files/activities/fiscal.

———. 2005. National decentralization policy. Kigali, Rwanda: Government of Rwanda. http://www.minaloc.gov.rw/doc/policy.

———. 2005. Paper on fiscal and financial decentralization policy. Kigali, Rwanda: Government of Rwanda.

———. 2004. Five years of decentralization implementation program (DIP). Kigali, Rwanda: Government of Rwanda.

Ministry of Public Service and Labor. 2004. Reconfiguration and transformation of Rwandan public administration: Strategies and implementation. Kigali, Rwanda: Government of Rwanda.

———. 2002. Policy framework for Rwanda's civil service reform. Kigali, Rwanda: Government of Rwanda.

———. 1997. Civil service reform: The true impact of retrenchment. *Insights* (September).

Ministry of Rehabilitation and Social Integration. 1995. Workshop on evaluation of rehabilitation resolution. Workshop paper. Kigali, Rwanda: Government of Rwanda.

Minogue, M. 1999. Power to the people? Good governance and the reshaping of the state. Public Policy and Management Working Paper 14, University of Manchester, IDPM.

———. 1998a. Is good governance a universal value? Public Policy and Management Working Paper 6, University of Manchester, IDPM.

———. 1998b. Changing the state: Concepts and practice in the public sector. Public Policy and Management Working Paper 4, University of Manchester, IDPM.

Moleketi, Geraldine. 2005. Speech by South African minister of public service and administration. http://www.african-union.org/Politicalaffairs.

Moses, Golola. 2003. The challenges to local bureaucracies in Uganda. Address to the Inter-University Council for Eastern Africa, Kampala, Uganda.

Msosa, C. P. 1998. Public sector reform: Malawi as a case study. Paper presented at the Eastern and Southern Africa Consultative Workshop, Arusha Tanzania. http://www.essentialaction.org/labor_report/malawi.html.

Mugabo, O. 2006. Adoption of Aid Policy by Cabinet.27 July. Government of Rwanda. Kigali, Rwanda. http://www.minecofin.gov.rw/en/inno-read_article .php?articleId=17&highlight=Economic%20reports.

Mugambage, F. 2005. Community policing in a post-conflict society: A case study of post-genocide Rwanda. PhD diss., University of Nairobi, Institute of Diplomacy and International Studies.Mugisha, Fred. 2006. *Building and information society, the case for Rwanda*. Washington, D.C.: Development Gateway Foundation.

Mukombozi, Robert, and Berna Namata. 2006. President's office sermons government planners. *New Times*, August 25.

Muliisa, Richard. 2006. Delegates clash over budget. *New Times*, September 14.

Musambayi, Katumanga. 2005. Towards an inclusive state: The politics of state reconstruction and reconstruction in Rwanda, 1994–2004. *Regional Development Dialogue* 26 (1).

Musoni, J. 2007. Budget speech, minister of finance and economic planning. 12 October. Government of Rwanda. Kigali, Rwanda. http://www.minecofin.gov .rw/en/inno-read_article.php?articleId=47&highlight=Economic%20reports.

Nation Newspaper Editorial. 2006. Kenya: A worthy civil service goal. *Daily Nation*, June 9.

NEPAD. 2005. NEPAD's e-school project kicks off in Rwanda. Kigali, Rwanda: NEPAD. http://www.nepad.gov.rw.

Niyitegeka, Gerald. 1995. Discussion on Rwanda's post genocide rehabiliation. May Relief Web. http://www.reliefweb.int/library/nordic/book4.

Nsibambi, Apollo. 2005. Africa day of administration and civil service and the United Nations Public Service. Uganda Management Institute speech, June 23, 2005.

Nzaramba, Stevenson, and Gertrude Majyambere. 2006. Economic development and poverty reduction strategy. *New Times*, February 9. http://www.rwanda gateway.org/article.php3?id_article=1579.

Obongo, S. 2000. Transferring new public management reforms: The case of civil service reforms in Kenya. PhD diss., University of Manchester, IDPM.

Olowu, D., and S. Sako, eds. 2002. *Better governance and public policy: Institutions for democratic renewal in Africa*. Bloomfield: Kumarian.

Olowu, et al. 1997. The role of the civil service in enhancing development and democracy: An evaluation of the Nigerian experience. Paper prepared for the conference on Civil Service Systems in Comparative Perspective, School of Public and Environmental Affairs, Indiana University, Bloomington, IN.

Omok, I. 2000. Old guards fighting hard. *New Africa* (387): 30–33.

Organization for Cooperation and Economic Development. 2002. Donor public service reform working groups. Development Cooperation Directorate: Development Assistance Committee. London. http://209.85.135.104/search?q =cache:Ae2uAXqhjYIJ:www.oecd.org/dataoecd/26/10/21677689.pdf+Donor +Public+Service+Reform+Working+Groups+held+in+London+on+April+22 –23,+2002,t&hl=en&ct=clnk&cd=1.

Osborne, D., and P. Plastrik. 1997. *Banishing bureaucracy: The five strategies for reinventing government.* New York: Penguin.

Owusu, Francis. 2005. Organizational culture, performance, and public reforms in Africa. Ghana case paper presented to the International Conference on Shared Growth in Africa, Accra, Ghana.

Peter, Lewis, ed. 1998. *Africa: Dilemmas of development and change.* Colorado: Westview Press.

Peters, Lucien. 1999. Downsizing the civil service in developing countries: Golden handshakes or smiling farewells? *Public Administration and development* (18): 381.

Polidano, C., M. Minogue, and D. Hulme. 2001. Why civil service reforms fail. Public Policy Management Working Paper 16, University of Manchester, IDPM.

———. 1999. The new public management in developing countries. Public Policy and Management Working Paper 13, University of Manchester, IDPM.

———. 1998. Conclusions: Looking beyond the new public management. In *Beyond the new public management: Changing ideas and practices in government*, ed. M. Minogue, C. Polidano, and D. Hulme. London, UK: Edward Elgar Publishing.

Rama, M. 1999. Public sector downsizing: An introduction. *World Bank Economic Review* 13 (1): 1–22.

Ratnam, Venkata, and Shizue Tomoda. 2005. *Practical guide for strengthening social dialogue in public service reform.* Geneva: ILO.

Rice, Xan. 2006. A mobile in every pocket is motto of tiny country aiming to be hub of technology. *New Times*, August 1, 2006.

Robinson, Mark. 2006. The Political economy of governance reforms in Uganda. Sussex, Brighton: Institute of Development Studies.

Rwanda Information Technology Agency. 2005. A review of the implementation of ICT. Report 4/NICI Plan P. Kigali, Rwanda: Government of Rwanda.

Sadig, R. 1996. Ethics and accountability in African civil service. *DPMN Bulletin* 3 (1).

Sandbrook, Richard, and Jay Oelbaum. 1999. *Reforming the political kingdom: Democratization and governance in Ghana's fourth republic.* Accra, Ghana: Institute of Economic Affairs.

Sharmini, Coorey, and Mark Plant. 2006. The joint staff advisory note of the poverty reduction paper annual progress report by the World Bank and the IMF, Washington, D.C.

Shihata, I. F. I. 1994. Administrative reforms in developing countries: Some general observations. In *Civil service reform in Latin America and the Caribbean: Proceedings of a conference*, ed. S. A. Chaudhry et al. Washington, D.C.: World Bank.

Smith, James M., ed. 2004. *A time to remember: Rwanda: Ten years after genocide.* Lound Hall, Bothamsall, Retford, Nottinghamshire, UK: Aegis Institute.

Smith, Russell. 2003. The impact of the hate media in Rwanda. *BBC Africa Online Journal.* http://news.bbc.co.uk/2/hi/africa/3257748.stm (accessed June 20, 2006).

Smoke, P., ed. 2001. African decentralization and local governance. *Public Administration and Development* 23 (1).

Stevens, M., and S. Teggemann. 2006. Comparative experience with administrative reform in Ghana, Tanzania, and Zambia. Paper presented at the World Bank Regional Workshop on Governance and Public Management, Johannesburg.

Tawfik, M. Rawi. 2003. *NEPAD and African development: Towards a new partnership between development actors in Africa*. Giza, Egypt: Cairo University.

Teskey, Graham, and Richard Hooper. 1999. Tanzania civil service reform programme: Case study, 5. http://unpauliI.unorg/intradoc/groups/public/documents.

Therkildsen, O. 2001. *Efficiency, accountability, and implementation: Public sector reform in eastern and southern Africa*. New York: United Nations University Press.

Thomas, L. Friedman. 2000. *Understanding globalization: The Lexus and the olive tree*. New York: Anchor Books.

Turner, M., and D. Hulme. 1997. *Governance, administration, and development: Making the state work*. Manchester, UK: Macmillan.

UNDP. 2004. Cultural liberty in today's diverse world. Human Development Report. http://www.undp.org/in/hdr2004/.

———. 2004. Rwanda country review on the role of ICT in poverty reduction in the achievement of the Millennium Development Goals (MDGs). New York: United Nations.

United Nations. 1995. UN fiftieth session, October 9. New York: United Nations. United Nations. 2001. World public sector report: Globalization and the state, pexecutive summary. New York: UN Headquarters.

USAID. 2003. The development challenge. Washington, D.C.: USAID. http://www.usaid.gov/pubs/cbj2003/afr/rw/.

U.S. State Department. 2001. State of Rwanda economy. Washington, D.C.: Government of United States. http://www.state.gov/r/pa/ei/bgn/2861.htm#econ.

Van der Heijden. 1999. Globalization, environmental movements, and international political opportunity structures. *Sage Journals On-Line*. Amsterdam: University of Amsterdam.

Vanessa, Harrhoff. 2005. Rwanda funds ICT development. Project; ICT Penetration in South Africa. Midrand. http://www.ictportal.org.za/archive.php.

Vuylsteke, Charles. 1988. Techniques of privatisation of state-owned enterprises. Vol. 1. Methods and Implementation, World Bank Technical Paper No. 88, World Bank.

Westcott, C. 1999. Guiding principals on civil service reform in Africa: An empirical review. *International Journal of Public Sector Management* 12 (2): 145–70.

World Bank. 2006. IMF and IDA report on Rwanda. http://www.worldbank.org/resources.

———. 1999. Operational document on economic recovery credit to Rwanda. Washington, D.C.: World Bank Public Information Centre.IDA/R99–135.

———. 1996. *Bureaucrats in business: The economic and politics of government ownership*. New York: Oxford University Press.

———. 1995. Mission de la banque mondiale: Réinstallation des réfugiés: Secteur education. Washington, D.C.: World Bank.

———. 1995. Rwandese republic emergency recovery project technical annex. January Report No. T- 6483-RW. Washington, D.C.: World Bank.

———. 1994. Rwanda assessment mission: Back-to-office september report. Washington, D.C.: World Bank.

———. 1994. Memorandum and recommendation of the president of the international development association to the executive directors on a proposed credit of SDR 35 million to the Rwandese Republic for an emergency recovery project. December Report No. P6483-RW. Washington, D.C.: World Bank.

———. 1989. *Sub-Saharan Africa: From crisis to sustainable growth*. Washington, D.C.: World Bank.

Zuckerman, Ethan. 2006. Cote d'Ivoire lurches towards civil war. http://www.ethanzuckerman.com.

Index

Ministries and programs are those of the Government of Rwanda, unless otherwise noted.